DEDICATION

This book is dedicated to...

The Lord Jesus Christ who is the Solid Rock on which I stand. He is the best thing that ever happened to me from the day I said "Yes, Lord" at the age of six years old.

To my parents: The credit for who I am today goes to them. So thanks to my dad and my dearly departed mother, Anganile Sakipuga Mwakasege, for demonstrating that "loving God is loving others."

To the Mwakasege children and the entire family. Your moral support helps me fulfill the Great Commission.

To all my friends in the Body of Christ. It is a blessing to count on your support.

To my husband George, and children Bupe and Ify. I pray that they will receive a double portion of the faith that God imparted to me even when I was a child growing up in my beautiful Tanzania.

Copyright © 2013 by
Dr. Nicku Kyungu Mordi | President and CEO
AFRICA Transformation Embassy

AFRICA Transformation Embassy
11247 Lockwood Dr. | Suite B | Silver Spring, MD 20901
T: 301.593.0333 | F: 301.593.0331 | www.atembassy.org

Contents

ACKNOWLEDGEMENTS

I t will not be possible to mention all the names of so many of you who have inspired my life over the years: thank you! May the Lord richly reward you.

I would however, like to thank Janet Getz whose typing brought this book into reality. Jane Merit Caldwell, you never gave up on me nor on the manuscript. You took it all over Oregon to find a publisher. Thank you for your faith. God has done it in spite of the obstacles—Praise Him!

Dr. Oral Roberts, for reading the manuscript and personally writing the Foreword. Indeed it was an honor to have had you as a friend and mentor. You are gone but not forgotten!

To Virene Cardenas, my editor and publisher. I am so glad I found you and so thankful for you. To Erica Thompson who did the initial editing, Jessica Chapman and Emily Wharton who edited the full manuscript, Raj Patel, IT Director and my creative Graphic Designer, and Khary D'Aguilar, for all his valuable IT skills. To a very special young man, Tony Chen: Your love for the Lord and His Word, your prayers and support always leave my heart happy every time I see you! To Blackwood Hills Publishing: You brought in all the many-faceted support I needed to bring this dream to reality…The Lord will not forget!

To my family in Tanzania and around the world. Let us continue to praise God for all He is to us. Frank, Bupe, Mama, Dad; though you are gone, this book is filled with memories of you. I wish you were here!!

Thanks also, to Pastor Hanfere Aligazi of The Ethiopian Evangelical Church in Washington D.C. who has graciously hosted Africa for Jesus Conferences from the very beginning. The Lord will certainly reward you. Finally, to my Pastor, and Chairman of the Board of International Gospel Outreach Ministries, Bishop Darlingston Johnson: You have been a true Under Shepherd, providing shelter and spiritual covering to so many! Thank you. Now to the Body of Christ: Without you I could not have experienced heaven on earth. Let us continue to fight the good fight of faith for His glory. I love you all and thank God for you.

FOREWORD

Nicku's life experiences are some of the most remarkable stories of faith I've ever heard.

Indeed, her faith is in many ways comparable to the faith talked about in Hebrews 11, particularly of Abraham's leaving home when God told him to go-- not knowing where he was going-- and having only his faith in God to lead him.

Nicku's faith is like the faith Daniel exhibited that protected him from the lions and like that which opened prison doors for Paul.

The miracles in this story are true—I have not a doubt. I know first-hand about some of them since I was President of Oral Roberts University when Nicku was a student there.

If Nicku Kyungu, a girl born in Tanzania, Africa can have faith to attend a charismatic university in the United States, believing God for all her expenses, and come out with three degrees, then surely "with God all things are possible."

Blind Faith—God's Amazing Miracles will stir your heart and let you know that if it happened to Nicku, then it can happen to you!

I see a great future for Nicku. The world has yet to see what God will do through a yielded vessel and as it does, it will never be the same again.

Evelyn and I truly recommend that you read this book. We believe that you will be glad you did.

Dr. Oral Roberts
Founder/Chancellor

Oral Roberts University
Tulsa, Oklahoma

INTRODUCTION

In the Gospel according to St. Luke, there is a story which is relevant to my situation. The story concerns Jesus Christ and the apostles. In Chapter 10, Jesus appointed seventy people to be His disciples. He commissioned them to go two-by-two into every city to preach the Gospel. The apostles listened to the instructions and assured their Master that they were ready to go. They bade each other farewell, said the last prayer, and departed.

They scattered to thirty-five cities. I can imagine them going forth in hope and faith to fulfill their mission. The apostles were able to heal the sick and to proclaim that the Kingdom of God was at hand (verse 9). They had greater or lesser successes, depending on the welcome they received in each town. Some cities received them warmly, others did not. In cities where they were not welcome, they were unable to fulfill their mission (verses 10 and 11). The apostles had to leave in disappointment. Nevertheless, they remained obedient to the commission to "Go."

After accomplishing their objective of healing the sick and proclaiming "The Kingdom of God is at hand," the seventy returned to Jesus with joy. They could not wait to share their mission experience with Jesus and with each other. As they shared their testimonies, Jesus perceived that their joy was related to the seeming success that they had experienced in the manifestations of the power that was given to them. He realized that they had missed the whole point of knowing who they were.

In Luke 20, Jesus talks of the power that believers have in Him. Then He gave them a principle that is applicable to all Christians. He told them not to rejoice because the evil spirits were subjected to them. That was not to be considered unusual since He had given them great power. Jesus wanted them to know that they were not to depend on physical circumstances to produce their joy, since circumstances changed all the time. That which the apostles needed to rejoice about was more important than casting out demons: they were to rejoice because their names were written down in heaven in the Lamb's Book of Life. That is what their joy should be based on.

Jesus was teaching them the same lesson He is teaching Christians today. Men and women of God who have been called out of darkness into His marvelous light are not to rejoice in external power, fame, or authority; but rather in the consciousness and knowledge that they are children of God. As you continue to read this book, know that you belong to God because you have believed in Jesus Christ, God's only begotten Son (John 3:16-18; Romans 10:8-11).

When you belong to God through Jesus Christ, your joy is based on the fact that your name is written in the Lamb's Book of Life. The joy of any Christian, therefore, should not depend on worldly possessions, abilities, accomplishments, successes or circumstances, but rather on knowing that you are God's special child. Your Heavenly Father loves you and you should love Him by obeying His Word and being available to do His will.

Most of my life I have tried to be available to God because I love Him. I rejoice knowing that God has total control to do whatever He wants with me and through me. This surrender was contingent upon my accepting Jesus Christ as my personal Lord and Savior, and upon the realization that I am God's child and my name has been written down in heaven.

Indeed, it was the greatest discovery to know that I was someone who belonged to Someone more powerful than anyone!

"Now if we are children, then we are heirs—heirs of God and co-heirs with Christ, if indeed we share in his sufferings in order that we may also share in his glory." (Romans 8:17)

Dr. Nicku Kyungu Mordi

WHAT OTHERS ARE SAYING ABOUT THIS BOOK

Although I have been God's servant for a number of years and have seen many moves of God, I was unaware of how cold my heart had grown up to the day that someone handed me "Blind Faith" to read. That night, I settled in my easy chair to read myself to sleep as I had become accustomed to doing in recent years. Not only was I feeling old age creeping upon me, but I was also having great difficulty falling asleep, and reading until my eyelids got heavy was the only effective sleep aid. This particular night, I settled in and began to read. Well, I read one chapter, then another, I felt new stirrings in my heart for the Lord. As I read the last sentence of the last chapter of the book, I realized that I had been with Jesus all night. I was jolted up from my chair with a "Hallelujah!" coming from deep within my soul. Over and over I cried, "Hallelujah." My faith was revived. My body lost all tiredness...all aches and pains were gone. I was "born again, again!" Whether you have been a christian for many years, or you are just getting to know Jesus, you MUST read this book. You won't want to put it down, once you start reading. It will change your life!

— *Pastor*
Germany

This sweet little book is destined to find its place among the Christian classics on Faith. The author draws you into her childlike faith from the first paragraph of her story, all the way to the very end. Not only is the reader gripped by the sweet simplicity of her faith, but the heart is left deeply stirred towards the Lord—to know Him more—to experience pure and simple faith in God and God alone! As someone who is faced with the realities of the daily physical, scientific world where faith is based on man's best efforts, I found this to be a soul-refreshing read!

— *Alicia J. Odum, M.D.*
(USA)

Is this an interesting read? You bet! Once I started reading this delightful book, I simply could not put it down. But it is so much more than a true page-turner....it is an absolute faith-builder! I started reading this book last night and never expected to spend the night with the Lord…reading and rejoicing! Waves of faith flooded my soul as the author revealed the reality and simplicity of Jesus. When morning light appeared at my window, I felt renewed in my faith. Every once in a while a special and unique book comes along that becomes a "best seller," not necessarily because of the standard book publishing and marketing strategies, but because it carries its own anointing from God. This is one of those! I appreciate the author's combination of real life supernatural and natural experiences interlaced with brief, but solid Christian teaching. I thought that was quite effective. As you read this charming, honest, "no guile" account of a little girl's faith that took her all the way from her homeland of Tanzania to the United States, you dear reader, will be moved to believe God for all He has for your life. All across the land, I can see believers' faith being ignited with a freshness and a wonder at God's amazing faithfulness as displayed in these pages. It will awaken your faith … pastor, parents, youth … all will benefit from reading this amazing book about our amazing God!

— *Morene D'Aguilar, Pastor*
Jamaica, West Indies

She is a powerful woman of God now; so I was told. But as a young person, I could relate to the child hearing from God at an early age. After I read this book, I got on my knees and rededicated my life to the Lord. I realize that the true reason I was born is to live for God. I am ready to go far away to serve the Lord, if that's what He wants. But my parents advised me to go to college and serve the Lord right in my dorm. I believe they are correct, and that is what I will do. I also believe that the author's intent was to share her testimonies with hopes that they will stir each reader's heart towards the Lord. She accomplished her goal in this reader. I am happy that my heart now belongs totally to Jesus; and whether near or far He calls me, "Jesus, I am available to You!"

— *A college-bound teenager*
Maryland, USA

.

Chapter 1

God's Call

One night when I was only six years old, I had a vivid dream that would affect my life forever. In the vision, I was sitting outside our house in Mbeya, Tanzania, washing smoke-blackened cooking pots using our homemade detergent—ashes mixed with sand and water. While I was washing the pots, a man dressed in a white kanzu (garment) came riding by on a motorcycle. I did not hear him until he rode right up. Stopping the engine, he called my name and said, "Nicku! Come, let us go together!" When I lifted my head to see who was talking, I recognized Him immediately. I don't know how, but I knew in my heart it was Jesus! The same Jesus in the Bible stories that my parents told me about! I did not answer Him except to say a word of greeting. I looked at His shining face in admiration and continued to wash the pots.

As He observed me, He said once again, "Nicku! Climb on the motorcycle and let us go!" Respectfully, I answered, "Sir, I cannot go. I have to do my work. These pots have to be washed before my parents come home." Then I lifted my head to look at Him and continued, "Besides, I cannot go with you without asking for my parents' permission."

I was taught not to go anywhere without parental approval, and I was careful to follow the rules. Going off with strange men was a particular taboo. Again Jesus called me, but I was afraid to go with a stranger without my parents' permission, yet He was so full of love. I really wanted to go with Him. I was torn. I remained with my head down, diligently cleaning the pot in my hands.

As a gentleman, Jesus decided to leave me alone. He started the motorcycle and was about to go when I shouted, "Please! Wait for me!" My heart was filled with love for Him. I did not want to see Him leave neither did I want to be left alone. "Let me go inside and wash my dirty hands and, at the same time, return these pots. Then I can come for a ride with you," I continued.

Jesus answered, "Nicku, you do not have to wash your hands. Just jump on the motorcycle and hold onto me tightly so you will not fall off." It was hard for me to decide what I wanted to do. I was ashamed to hold on to His white garment with dirty hands, and I also was afraid of my parents' rod if I left home without their permission. Still, I was so interested in Him that I did not want Him to leave me. He felt like a friend, and since He even knew my name, it was more difficult for me to let Him go. He had a unique personality. It was attractive, and I wanted to know Him.

> *"... He appears like the dawn, fair as the moon, bright as the sun, majestic as the stars in procession."* (Song of Solomon 6:10)

While I was still undecided, He started riding away. I knew He would leave me if I attempted to go inside to clean my hands. My heart started throbbing. I looked at the moving motorcycle and suddenly dropped the pots and ran after Him. When He saw me, He slowed down and I jumped onto the passenger's seat behind Him. As I rode with Him, I was overjoyed. Nothing mattered anymore. My heart was at peace.

We rode without saying anything. Amazingly, I was content. I did not think about anything except that I was enjoying the ride. Then suddenly I remembered my dirty hands. I did not wash them after cleaning the pots. I glanced at them quickly and could not believe my eyes— my hands were clean! I looked at His garment, and it was as white as it was before. *What happened to the dirt on my hands?* I could not believe it. For a while my mouth remained open in pure amazement!

Pots used on firewood are normally very black from the smoke. The cleaning detergent, which consists of ashes, sand, water, and the black soot on the pot, creates a black, messy, tar-like substance. I knew how dirty my hands were, and now to see them so clean without washing them was so peculiar. I could not figure out why my hands did not make His white garment dirty. It was an unsolvable mystery; nevertheless, I did not say a word. Indeed, Jesus had washed all my sins away. That was my only conclusion.

After a while, we came to a valley between two villages, Ilomba and Luanda. There I saw thousands of people from all cultures in all sizes and colors. When we approached the crowd, they all knew Jesus. They gave Him respectful gestures but did not speak to Him. Jesus said to me, "Nicku, you stay here while I go do something else." Then He added, "Feel at home here." His face lit up as He spoke to me, and I felt so happy to be there. Everyone was busy talking with each other without any fear. It was a place of peace and friendliness. People seemed to enjoy mingling. It was a reception or party of some kind. Though no one spoke with me, I did not mind. I was completely at home.

> *"Consequently, you are no longer foreigners and aliens, but fellow citizens with God's people and members of God's household."* (Ephesians 2:19)

Most of the time my eyes were fixed on Jesus as he moved about. Sometimes I would look at the different people and admire the variety of costumes. Then my eyes would glance through the crowd to find Jesus. When I found him in the crowd, my heart would be filled with joy. Although there were many people, Jesus was easily seen because of the shining white garment that He was wearing. His presence was unique; He was tall and His movements commanded attention. There was a charisma about Him as He walked around. No one could confuse or refuse to acknowledge His presence.

Within me I kept saying, "There is Jesus; there is Jesus," as if I was pointing to Him with my spirit. I would admire the people but continued to fix my eyes on Him. "There is Jesus, the man who brought me here, and the only One who talked to me and with me." These thoughts did not leave my spirit. Indeed, there is no friend like Jesus.

At one point, when I tried to fix my eyes on Jesus, I could not find Him. I panicked and screamed, "Where is Jesus?" I shouted, "Mama, Mama, where has Jesus gone?" I glanced through the crowd, but He was not there. Fear and anxiety gripped me. I did not want to lose Him. "Where is He?" I cried aloud. "I do not see Him. Where is Jesus?"

I continued to shout and cry. As I ran through the crowd, I felt like I jumped out of something. I soon realized that I had jumped out of my bed (we were three, sometimes four, children sharing one bed). As I left the bed, I met Dad in the hallway.

"What is the matter, Nyambilila?" he asked, taking me in his strong arms. ["Nyambilila" was my grandmother's name. He always used it to express affection or concern for my siblings and me.] "You must be having a bad nightmare." I protested, "It was not a nightmare, Daddy. It was a party with Jesus."

"What party?" he asked. He took me into their bedroom so I could talk with him and my mother. He repeated the question, "Nicku, what party are you talking about?" I told them about how I met Jesus and went to a party with Him. They gave me a questioning look. I continued to cry and tried to convince them that it was not a dream or a nightmare. My dad told me I was having a vision.

The word "vision" was foreign to me, and it never occurred to me that it was night and everyone was asleep. "When Jesus called me, I was not asleep," I insisted. "He talked with me." Then I looked at my mother and said, "Please, Mama, I want Jesus. Why did He leave me?" It was a cry of sincerity and desperation from a six-year-old. The impression Jesus made on me was irresistible. I wanted to be where He was all the time. When they could not give me an answer, I continued to cry.

My parents could not sleep. They kept me in their bed hoping I would be convinced it had all been a dream. Unfortunately, I refused to accept my mother's reasoning because it was so real to me. I ended up falling asleep sometime later without realizing it. But when I woke early in the morning, I went outside, faced Ilomba, and started to cry all over again, wishing Jesus would come with His motorcycle.

I was quite unhappy for several days. I wanted to be with Jesus. Sometimes I would take the pots outside even if they weren't dirty, hoping Jesus would show up. My mother prayed for me and several times she would say, "Nicku, do not be unhappy. If you will be a good girl and live for God, Jesus will take you, not only to Ilomba and Luanda, but He will take you all over the world to see those people you met in your vision. Jesus is able to take you to them if you will love Him."

Her advice did not help much at the time. I did not want to wait until I grew up to be with Jesus. Besides, I wasn't sure what was required to be "a good girl." I wanted to be with Jesus now! As the weeks passed by, I forgot about the vision and started living normally again. However, deep within me, I knew that one day Jesus would come back for me, and we would ride together once again.

Chapter 2

Born Again

Although I was called a Christian, I did not know the importance of studying the Word of God for myself, nor what it meant to be "born again." My denomination baptized us when we were babies, and we were confirmed when we were teenagers. The terminology "being born again" was emphasized during baptismal services but never referred to in day-to-day living. Concerning the Word, I often thought it was only the so-called born-again people who were supposed to read the Word of God, not the Christians. It was like they were two different groups of Christian people, the "born-again" Christians and the "regular" Christians. It wasn't until later that I came to understand what "born-again Christian" meant.

In those days, I used to think that as long as I went to church and was called a Christian that it was good enough. My father read his Bible every day. In the evenings, the entire family had a Bible study. I felt that was all I needed. Today, many are still being taught that when you are baptized and confirmed and attend a Bible study, you are a Christian. Some think that if they have devoted parents who study the Word of God, it will account for their personal salvation. Not so! As I learned, you must be born again (John 3:3).

"If you believe in your heart and confess with your mouth that Jesus is Lord, you shall be saved." (Romans 10:9)

My father was a minister in God's vineyard and my mother loved God and showed love to everyone. Coming from such a God-fearing background, I was naturally regarded as a born-again Christian because people could at least observe my morals and character, which were influenced by a Christian home. My life revolved around loving the church, loving people, and wanting to help anybody at anytime. I was a "good" person who committed only minor infractions like engaging in harmless sibling rivalry or taking sugar to mix with water in order to have a sweet drink. Although I knew I was not supposed to do this, I did it in secret every time I got the chance. Yet people thought I was a good girl. But the Bible says,

"If we claim to be without sin, we deceive ourselves and the truth is not in us." (John 1:8)

In the Old Testament it also says,

"...all our righteousness is as filthy rags." (Isaiah 64:6)

In us, there is no goodness regardless of how others perceive us. Indeed, when people considered my good moral conduct and my devotion to the church, they thought I was a good Christian and an example to others. However, according to what Isaiah 64:6 tells us, that is not Biblical; I just did not know any better. The Bible is full of scriptures indicating that we are not declared righteous by observing the law (Romans 3:20) but by faith in Jesus Christ (Romans 3:24, 5:1).

As soon as I learned how to read, I began to study the Word of God in my simple child-like way. Later, as a twelve-year-old, I remember praying and wishing I could understand several things that I had read in the Bible. They were so intriguing, and I wanted to know. I even wrote down prayers that I read often. One of those prayers was to know God and live for Him. I prayed that prayer often without understanding its full implication.

One day, the Holy Spirit revealed to me my need to be "born again." Someone, or something, was prompting me to confess Jesus as my personal Lord and Savior. The Holy Spirit went on to tell me that I needed to commit my life fully to God. I could not understand why since I had already been baptized and confirmed. Above all, I knew I had committed my life to Jesus since the age of six when

I fell in love with Him after the vision He had given me. However, I knew I had not confessed that I was a sinner.

That day, the Spirit of God continued to urge me to confess. He prompted me, and I knelt down and confessed that I was a sinner (without understanding what it truly meant). I even mentioned the sugar I took that no one knew about. My prayer was sincere, and I felt like someone was approving my confession. The room did not feel empty. It felt like an angelic host was there witnessing my adoption as a daughter of the Most-High God (Romans 8:14-17). I had an indescribable feeling of joy afterward. I told my parents what I did. I also wanted others to have the same experience—to know without a shadow of doubt that their sins were forgiven.

I started encouraging others to become born-again Christians even though I did not have any understanding of the Scripture to help me. When they asked how, I just said, "Listen to your heart. Someone will tell you that you are a sinner and that you need to confess all your sins and surrender your life to Him." I believe God's Spirit took over because some of my friends were convicted and were saved. God heard their confession and forgave them and their lifestyles changed. Although I did not even know how to lead them in the sinner's prayer, God knew. All I could tell them was what I had experienced. It might not have been theologically sound, but it worked.

There are times when God transforms people without using the traditional Christian methodology. He is God, and we cannot contain Him in our church programs. He goes far beyond that. He wants us to be open and available to Him. Jesus demonstrated this when He talked with the Samaritan woman at the well. The woman had a personal encounter with Christ. She went around telling others about her experience (Read John 4:29, 39-42). People were changed and Jesus became the center of their lives. The story of the Samaritan woman has inspired me to share Jesus's love without any fear.

Chapter 3

Alone, But Not Alone!

I am very grateful to God for the many miracles He has done in my life. It is a daily excitement for me to depend on God and trust in His Word. Faith in God has released miracles and given me a joy that does not depend on material things but on the realization that I am God's child. I cannot tell you in this short book all of what faith in God has done in my life. What I want to share is only a fraction of the things God has done and can do if you will fully trust and depend on Him. The Bible says:

> *"Now to Him who is able to do immeasurably more than all we ask or imagine, according to his power that is at work within us...."* (Ephesians 3:20)

You can have God's power within you to tap into all that God has for you. One of God's miracles occurred when my sister Josephine and I went to stay with our uncles, who were living near the jungles far from the city. Many people lived there because they had a gold mine inside the jungles. Although they were nice and kind to us, I did not like to live with them because there was no church. I cannot remember how many times I begged my sister to leave, but she refused. When our return date came, my sister wanted to stay longer because there was no one to escort us home. But after my persistence, we left. I had no fear of anything. I wanted to leave in order to go to church, even if it meant walking alone in the jungle.

As soon as we reached the dangerous part of our trip, fear gripped my sister and she decided to go back to our uncles' place. She was certain I would not travel alone because the forest had all kinds of wild animals. It was dangerous for two young girls to walk by themselves without a weapon. But I had no fear; I kept walking. She pleaded with me to go back to find someone to make the two-hour walk with us through the jungle. My head was raised up high as I walked. I did not want to listen or look back. I continued to walk on ahead of her, longing to be in the church that evening.

After a while, I did not hear my sister talking. I thought she was too afraid to call me to slow down in case the noise awakened the animals. But before I knew what happened, I heard a sound and realized I was face to face with a wolf! I ran so fast that a piece of my clothing fell off. After the wolf disappeared, I turned to look for my sister but she was nowhere to be seen. I became frightened because I still had a long way to go through the forest. A voice within me said, "Don't look back again. Go on, I am with you."

Confidence came and I started running and walking. I arrived home, miraculously, and no one could believe I walked alone from my uncles' gold mine to Chunya City Center. God had indeed protected me.

Meanwhile, my sister arrived back at my uncles' house and told them I refused to return with her. They became concerned for my safety and immediately started to look for me. They followed the path we had taken earlier and found my clothing. Assuming animals had killed me, they were horrified and started crying and searching for me in hopes of finding some of my remains. They searched until it was dark and returned home in order to continue at daybreak.

At this point, two of my cousins were told to go inform my parents that I was killed and there was no trace of my body except for a piece of my clothing. Although it was night, my sister still had to travel with them. The men took spears to protect themselves from wild animals. When they arrived at my home, we were fast asleep. My parents were awakened and told, "We have sad news. Nicku is dead." My parents broke out laughing because I was alive and well and asleep in my room! God had protected me. The Scripture says,

"The Lord is my Shepherd, I shall not want. He makes me lie down in green pastures. Even though I walk

through the valley of the shadow of death, I will fear
no evil, for you are with me...." (Psalm 23: 1-2, 4)

As Christians, our hope while we are on this pilgrimage should be in Jesus. One songwriter wrote, "Stand up for Jesus, stand in His strength alone, the arm of flesh will fail you, ye dare not trust your own." On our own, we cannot do anything. We need to depend on God. The Scripture in John 15:5 commands us to abide in the Vine—that Vine is Jesus Christ. Then we will reach our potential to fulfill God's plan for our lives.

Trials and temptations are not eliminated when we walk in the faith of God. The difference is that when we have God in us, we will be walking above all the trials and temptations. Situations and circumstances can affect our happiness but not our joy. Christ won that joy for us when He died on the cross and said, "It is finished" (John 19:30). Indeed, Jesus paid it all for us.

Having this assurance of victory from a young age, I greet each day with reverence for the opportunities it contains. I meet people with a smiling face and love in my heart—all for the glory of Christ. Faith in God has given me confidence to stand for Christ wherever I am, no matter what the circumstances. Let us live by faith and not by sight (2 Corinthians 5:7). Remember to put God first in everything (Proverbs 3:6,4). Trusting God in every area of our lives is not easy, but it is worth it, no matter what the cost. Indeed, salvation is free but not cheap.

As human beings, we will face hurtful or unpleasant situations and circumstances. At times, situations will require us to act with logic or within the reality of our society, but as children of God who have been redeemed by the blood of Jesus Christ, we must be sensitive to God's leading. God can help us rise above those difficult circumstances. We can have peace in the midst of a storm because our God is bigger than all of our problems.

Chapter 4

My Trip to India

As a sixteen-year-old student of the Msalato Secondary School in Dandoma, Tanzania, receiving a letter from the Juliette Low World Friendship Fund of the United States of America was a dream (Juliette Low was the founder of the Girl Scouts Association). The letter informed me that I was selected to go to Poona, India, as a representative of the Tanzanian Girl Guides Association. When I read the letter, I did not believe it was possible. There is no junk mail in Tanzania, so I knew it wasn't junk. I just dismissed it as a mistake. I put the letter aside without thinking much about it.

Two months passed, then another letter came from the Girl Guides headquarters in Dar es Salaam, the capital city of Tanzania. The commissioner of the association sent her congratulations on being selected as their representative. The letter went on to say, "I hope you are getting ready for your trip, so please let us know if you need anything." Still, I could not believe it; I thought it was a big joke. I was not able to tell anyone about it except my friend, who agreed that it was a mistake.

Often, other girls used to think my life was very peculiar. If I shared any of God's miracles, they thought I made them up. To share that letter was to invite them to tease me, so I was careful about what I shared. One day, my school headmistress called me to her office. She wanted to make some arrangements concerning schoolwork when I left for the trip. Then I finally believed the trip was real, but I still did not know what to do or how to prepare for it. Even my teachers did not help me; they all assumed I knew what to do because I did not seek their help.

Since I did not start preparing when I first got the news, months of preparation time was wasted. I now had to do everything in a rush. One month before the trip, I got another letter and a ticket requiring me to arrive at the Girl Guides headquarters two weeks before leaving for India so I could meet with the other candidate and the association leaders. Excitement came over me, and I could not stop talking about the trip. Everyone wanted to know how I was selected. When I told them it was God, they did not believe it, and I did not try to convince them.

The time came to leave Dodoma for Dar es Salaam. It was a two-day journey by train. When I arrived, I stayed with my cousins. We talked most of the night. The following day, I went to the headquarters. No one could believe how unprepared I was. They had to get a traveling document because there was not time to apply for a passport. Others had to lend me some of their national costumes since I had none. I was unprepared but very happy to go overseas. I had no idea what an overseas trip entailed, but that was part of the excitement and learning.

My sister flew with me to Nairobi, where the other candidate and I connected for our flight to India. When we landed in Bombay, we had to travel by train to Poona. I cannot recall how many hours we rode, but I vividly remember all the poor people lying in the streets and between the highways. The sight of such poverty made me cry all the way to Sangam. Other delegates from Europe and America could not understand why I could not relate to them. "You are an African. You must be used to poverty," they commented.

Their comments did not bother me. I knew they would understand one day. After a few days, they realized it was true—I was not used to poverty. Not every African is surrounded by jungles or poverty. Some of the delegates from Europe and America told me they changed their opinions and were re-evaluating their knowledge about Africa. It was shocking for me to see people in the misery of poverty yet still see people living in extreme luxury. The gap between the poor and rich was too great in India.

At this Girl Guide Jamboree, twenty-seven delegates represented ten different countries. From the continent of Africa, the only Tanzanians were an Indian girl, Shamin, from Dar es Salaam, and myself. When the delegates thought of anything about Africa, they automatically addressed me rather than Shamin. (Stereotypically, I appeared more African than the Indian girl Shamin.)

The experiences in India were very educational for all of us. The people were friendly and hospitable. They invited us to their homes, and I enjoyed their spicy food and admired their extended family ties.

It was fascinating to see how devoted the Indian people were to their religious rituals. Most of the families we visited were Hindus. Every home had a special place where they burnt candles and offered prayers to their gods. I learned that Hindus believed their gods lived in the house, and every family had a special place to worship.

How many of us Christians have a family altar? I could not help thinking as the families explained Hinduism to me.

We attended the Diwali festival, which symbolizes the triumph of good over evil. It also was a time to welcome Lakshmi, the Hindu goddess of wealth. Before the festival, most of the people would take oil baths to purify themselves in order to welcome their gods. It was very educational.

However, the highlight of the trip was the visit to the caves and temples in the Islands of the Elephants, located in the Arabian Sea. To reach the islands, we went by boat and then had to walk barefoot. We had to climb over 180 steps just to visit the temple where the Hindu god Shiva lived. It was a very exhausting experience.

I will never forget what our tour guide told me when I complained about how tired I was. "If you want to meet with the gods and have your needs met, you have to suffer going up, then they will hear you," he said. "There are some people who climb these steps on their knees in desperation for their prayers to be heard by the gods."

Still knowing little about Hinduism, this was hard for me to understand. While I respected their belief, I had a difficult time relating since I worshiped a God who accepted me and gave me my heart's desires even when I did something wrong. The people who made that trek were truly devoted. I felt bad that they had to go through such pain to have a prayer answered and found myself thanking my God that He did not require that much of me. He sees my heart's desires, and He answers my prayers in a different way.

Shiva is a well-known Hindu god. He is the king of the dancers. In some statues, he appears with three heads, which symbolizes him as the destroyer, preserver, and creator. There are many other Hindu gods with different functions. As I walked around looking at the sacrifices people left, the tour guide explained what each god and the sacrifices meant. Despite my interest in Hinduism, I found myself very sad. The reason was two-fold. One, I was tired of going up 180 steps without shoes. Two, I felt sad for the people, who, while very sincerely looking for

God, I believed were looking in the wrong places. The Bible says,

"How then, can they call on the one they have not believed in? And how can they believe in the one of whom they have not heard? And how can they hear without someone preaching to them?" (Romans 10:14)

Nevertheless, I could not open my mouth to share about my God, the ever-present reality of my life. I was warned several times before the trip not to witness to anyone because that would be breaking the law. They told us that the punishment was death for anyone who preached on the holy islands. Hinduism was heavy on my heart, though, and I was thankful my God heard me as I sought his direction silently.

"But know that the Lord hath set apart him that is godly for himself. The Lord will hear when I call unto him." (Psalms 4:3)

All throughout India, I was warned many times not to share my faith in God. There were times when I could not participate in an activity because I violated the rule by sharing about Jesus and His saving grace. It wasn't that I deliberately disobeyed their rules. But sometimes I could feel God's love so passionately that it became overwhelming. I could feel his love, peace, and joy so abundantly that I could not contain myself. I just wanted to share what I felt.

I was grounded often because I kept talking about my God and Savior, Jesus Christ. I did not intentionally decide to break the law. It happened because Jesus's love was what I really loved to talk about. The Bible says,

"... For out of the abundance of the heart the mouth speaketh." (Matthew 12:34)

My heart is consumed with God's love and sharing it with others anywhere.

On the day we visited the island and walked around the temples, my heart felt heavy with God's love and compassion for the people. Even the promise of severe punishment could not have prevented me from sharing the Living God, but the reality was that I was too tired to even open my mouth. I went around without even a word; I could not even comment on anything we saw. However, in my spirit, I kept thanking God. I was so grateful He came to me, and I did not have to go up to Him. God never asks us to go to His level. Instead, He comes and meets us where we are and helps us walk by faith, a step at a time, in order to be transformed in His image.

In the temple, when I heard people calling on their gods, I called on God in my spirit. He was the one name I knew—the name of Jesus, who is above every other name. As a Christian, I knew what would happen if they did not find God. So while watching them call on their gods, I was interceding for the many who were perishing for lack of knowledge. It is the same burden I have today:

"Go into all the world and preach the Good News to all creation...." (Mark 16:15)

Among the delegates who said they were Christians, I discovered some were churchgoers only. I had the opportunity to share with them about God's love and what it meant to have a personal relationship with Christ. I prayed with them for their spiritual understanding and I know God answered many of our prayers. One girl accepted Christ as her Lord and Savior. Some often called me to pray for their needs. I was like their spiritual delegate. Others loved to ask me about Africa or tell me what they knew about Africa and the people. Their perception was usually distorted.

Around the campfire, I would tell them what I knew about my country and the people and then I would change the subject. "Instead of talking about Africa," I would say, "Let us talk about the important issue. What does it mean to be a Christian?" Then I would talk about God. Sometimes I would sing about Jesus who saves, who keeps, and who satisfies. Some would leave because they weren't interested in hearing about God, but others would stay and ask questions, then I would end with a prayer. It was a blessing to fulfill my favorite Scripture, *"I am not ashamed of the Gospel of Jesus Christ."* (Romans 1:16)

When our trip came to an end, many thanked me for making a difference in their lives, culturally and spiritually. The separation was very emotional. Nevertheless, I looked forward to going back to school. When I arrived at school, it was unbelievable. I had become a celebrity. However, my experience did not change my attitude toward anyone. I told my friends that it was God who had opened the door for me to go overseas. And when I pondered on all that the Lord accomplished in me and through me while I was away, I had to admit that, indeed, He had purposefully selected me. Friends at school still thought I had otherworldly connections.

"I know this is just a beginning," I told them. "God will take me to other countries all over the world." Years later, this would prove to be a prophetic statement about my life. God is still taking me around His world.

Chapter 5

Mending a Refrigerator

Some situations in life are so mundane that we think involving God would be unnatural. Sometimes we tend to assume God is only interested in our spiritual well-being or physical health and not much concerned with our belongings, like furniture and other possessions. We forget God is not limited in what He can do. He is concerned with all of our needs.

In the story of Elisha and the floating axhead from Kings 6:1-7, the children of God wanted to build a larger meeting place. One of them borrowed an ax to cut down the trees by the Jordan River. As they worked, the axhead fell in the water and they could not find it. Elisha, a man of God, prayed for a miracle and the axhead floated to the surface. Scientifically, heavy objects sink. So naturally, the axhead sank to the bottom of the Jordan. Then Elisha prayed and a miracle was manifested. God is more powerful than any scientific principle, especially when His child dares to believe in the impossible. God is above all!

As a young adult, I found this principle to be very real. In 1974, I was living in the capital city of Dar es Salaam, which is generally very hot and humid. At that time, I was renting two rooms in a house on a hill facing the Jangwani football grounds. The house had six rooms, and other tenants were occupying the other four. I shared the two rooms with my two sisters, Rehema and Bupe, who were living with me. At the time this miracle occurred, I also had three visitors—one of my elder sisters and two friends.

The place was always crowded with visitors, and I loved it. The house did not have any kind of air conditioning except the natural breeze. At night, it was cool because we slept with the windows open. It was hot during the day and we would drink lots of water, as well as juices on special occasions. There was nothing like having a cold soft drink or cold water from the refrigerator.

With guests at home, it was a bad time for my refrigerator to break down, but it did. For four days, I called different electricians to diagnose the problem. They all said it was not repairable. I took it to the embassy's repairman, and he told me the same thing: "Nicku, this refrigerator is beyond repair. New parts are needed." He looked at me and concluded, "But you know it is not possible to get new parts in this country. Just forget it and start getting used to doing without." The broken refrigerator was one I had bought in Nairobi, Kenya, where I worked before moving to Dar es Salaam to work with a foreign mission. But he was right. The parts I needed to fix my refrigerator were not available anywhere in the country. The electrician said that I should just forget about ever using that refrigerator again. It was broken and useless.

I gave up and felt sorry for my visitors. The weather was so hot and humid, and they were uncomfortable, not having anything cold to drink, but nothing could be done about it. My younger sisters Rehema and Bupe were also very uncomfortable; we were not used to being without a refrigerator. At that time, however, we were more concerned for our visitors from Europe. I tried everything I could to fix that refrigerator, but it seemed impossible. Then I started to believe in a miracle. I prayed and trusted God for another refrigerator. It never occurred to me to trust God to fix the one I had.

Six days later as we slept, I heard a voice in my spirit say, "Nicku, do you want to mend your refrigerator?" I tried to open my eyes but could not. "Of course I want my refrigerator to work," I answered.

"Then mend it!" the voice said. "I do not know anything about mending it or about electricity," I replied.

Then a diagram appeared in front of me. The voice started giving me instructions on how to do the job while a hand pointed at different parts of the diagram. As I listened,

I was trying to open my eyes to look but something kept them closed.

When the voice finished, the hand disappeared for a while and everything was quiet, as if someone was waiting for my action. Then, as if someone was standing a few inches from my face, the voice said, "Do you understand what to do?" Still puzzled about what was happening, I answered, "Yes, sir!" Then the voice said, "What are you waiting for? Go and mend the refrigerator!" I jumped off the bed as if someone was pushing me. Immediately, I knew it was a vision and shouted, "Thank you, Lord," and went to the living room.

I was sleeping with my sister Enjo on the same bed, and the other two sisters were on the mattress on the floor—four adults in one room. Two men (the visitors from Europe) were asleep in the living room where the refrigerator was. I got off the bed, rushed to the sitting room, and turned on the light without any fear of waking up those who were asleep.

"Nicku, what is going on?" they asked when the bright light woke them. I said confidently, "I am going to mend the refrigerator."

"At this time of the night?!" they shouted with wonder.

"Yes, because God has shown me how to do it." They shook their heads and pulled the covers over their heads. They did not ask any more questions. Two of my sisters in the other room also got up to see what was happening.

Sometimes my family could not understand me. Some concluded that I would go crazy if I did not slow down. They always said I was a fanatic about the things of God. Others thought there was something different about me, especially about my relationship with God, but they could not pinpoint what it was. Whenever I said, "God has told me something," it usually happened. God talked to me in different ways, and they could not understand or argue about it. Many times I could not understand either, except to obey and follow what God was saying.

That night was one of those times when they considered me "crazy" and "strange" but kept silent. Those who were awake came around to watch me. I struggled to turn the refrigerator around. When I saw the wires, I started mending it. I could hear them whispering, "What is she going to do?" I did not pay any attention and just followed the instructions that God had given me.

I looked at the wires when the refrigerator was turned around and was surprised to see that everything I saw in the diagram had been real and very clearly marked. It was like God put new parts in. It was so easy to do. I felt like an electrician. It was exciting, especially when others were watching. I used a table knife to screw and unscrew something according to the instructions, as well as other more technical things. When I finished, I turned the power on and the refrigerator started to function in just a few moments.

I screamed, "Praise the Lord! It is working!" My family came back to look closely to see if it was true. Our God is real, and it is wonderful to obey Him. I am sure you can imagine what followed that night. We did not go back to sleep. The miracle shout woke the neighbors up, and they came to see what had happened. When they found out, they started praising and thanking God with us. His love and care for our daily concerns were demonstrated that night.

The following day, I went to the office and told the story to everyone who said my refrigerator was never going to work again. I shared about the vision and the diagram. Of course, they could not believe it. Some came and saw, and, in spite of seeing that something supernatural had taken place, they still could not believe. They suggested that my visitors from Europe had brought the new parts. I did not try to persuade them to believe because it was beyond man's comprehension. Nevertheless, their unbelief could not erase the reality of what we experienced. Indeed, the things of God are foolishness to a carnal man.

The miracle was so great that we kept on talking about it. Some who did not believe started making up stories to discredit it, while many who did not believe in the God of miracles became Christians. People accepted Jesus Christ and fell in love with His mysterious ways. I had more opportunities to witness to both my Muslim and Christian neighbors. They came to see the refrigerator, and I had to position it where people could see the back of it.

Our God is faithful. We need to trust Him in everything. Today, you can understand why I often say, "My God really cares for everything in my life. He is my all in all." I thank Him, and I want to serve Him with all my heart. God is more concerned about you than anyone else could ever be. It is His promise to care for you if you will believe in Him and obey Him. The Bible says,

"Humble yourselves, therefore, under God's mighty hand, that he may lift you up in due time. Cast all your anxiety on him because he cares for you." (1 Peter 5:6-7)

That "miracle refrigerator" (as named by the neighborhood) continued to work for a long time. In 1977, when I left Tanzania to obey God's call for a mission assignment to Sweden, I gave it to my brother Grant. My sister, who was visiting her family at the time and saw me repair it, told me she has never forgotten that night. From time to time she would say, "Nicku, the miracle refrigerator is functioning strong." It was a powerful testimony in itself. God is real. I thank Him for choosing me and revealing Himself to me in so many ways.

As human beings, we should not try to understand everything that God does. Our responsibility is to obey Him. What does not make sense to us, makes sense to Him. He is our creator. We need to be in tune with Him and say, "Yes" to His way. Believe when He says, *"For I know the plans I have for you, . . . plans to prosper you*

and not to harm you, plans to give you hope and a future."
(Jeremiah 29:11)

Chapter 6

Mission Call to Sweden

Although I was a secretary by profession, I found ministering to others to be far more fulfilling. The Bible says,

> *"Whatever your hand finds to do, do it with
> all your might, for in the grave, where you are
> going, there is neither working nor planning nor
> knowledge nor wisdom."* (Ecclesiastes 9:10)

I tried to demonstrate God's love to every person with whom I came in contact. Witnessing to others was part of my lifestyle. I tried to get to know those who did not know Christ in order to share God's saving grace. I challenged them to discover His love and power by accepting Him as their personal Lord and Savior.

As a young girl, I did not have the normal life other working girls enjoyed. My free time was consumed with fulfilling God's commission. On weekends and during vacation, God sent me to different parts of East Africa, namely Kenya, Uganda, and Tanzania, to share the gospel. Many times it was not easy, but, nevertheless, I obeyed.

"But you keep your head in all situations, endure hardship, do the work of an evangelist, discharge all the duties of your ministry." (2 Timothy 4:5)

I came from a large family and no one held a paying job except for my sister. Being the second person in my family to receive a salary, it was a natural thing to help the others financially. Until I got a job, I lived with my sister, who was the sole financial supporter for my family at that time.

It was a blessing to start working after school. I stayed four years with my sister in Nairobi. I left the job in Kenya and moved back to Tanzania to work with the American Embassy. Two of my younger sisters came to live with me in Dar es Salaam, and I had to support them and send them to private school.

Despite these financial difficulties, I used every opportunity to evangelize. The small salary I received accomplished so many things. It paid for our upkeep, and

I even sent some home to help other relatives. It was used to help pastors and other ministries, too. As a leader of our church with a good job, God provided many opportunities to help those in need.

In 1977, I felt in my spirit that God was calling me to do something different. He was calling me to give up all for the sake of the Gospel. I could not understand. As far as I was concerned, I knew I had given up most things. My social life was very different from other girls. All I loved to do was to share Christ with others. What Paul said in Philippians 1:21 was a reality, "For to me, to live is Christ and to die is gain." People used to call me names like "Mother Superior" and "Jesus Woman." I certainly did not act superior to anyone but they just felt that I was different. Those names did not bother me. I knew who I was in Christ and my life was dedicated to Him.

"Blessed are you when people insult you and persecute you and falsely say all kinds of evil against you because of Me." (Matthew 5:11)

There was a special understanding between the Lord and me, knowing that my life was considered peculiar and abnormal in the eyes of many. I felt so "normal" in my relationship with God! Others did not understand how I claimed to enjoy life by spending all my time talking about God. Even today, many people do not understand that true, real life is living for God. The Bible calls us to be "a chosen people, a royal priesthood, a holy nation, a people belonging to God, that you may declare the praises of Him who called you out of darkness into His wonderful light" (1 Peter 2:9).

For two weeks in May 1977, I kept hearing one word in my spirit, "Go." This word, however, was not new to me. I was preaching all the time. Any time God said, "Go," I was ready to say, "Yes, Lord, where?" Then He would direct me. But this time is wasn't as clear. I was scared of what he would say. As I sought His face, I heard in my inner spirit, "I am calling you to go farther than East Africa. Go and serve me far away."

I thought I had already been serving Him far away. I was serving Him in my hometown, in the local region, in my country, and in neighboring countries. I felt I had fulfilled being His witness "in Jerusalem, and in all Judea and Samaria, and to the ends of the earth" (Acts 1:8). So I did not understand how far he meant by "far away."

I tried to brush the idea away, thinking it was imagination only, but I could not and knew God was speaking. I started fasting and praying. As I prayed about it, I shared with my pastor and requested some of my prayer partners to pray with me. I wanted God to reveal where He wanted me to go or what He wanted me to do.

In June 1977, the answer to our prayer came. God spoke clearly, "Go to Sweden and witness for Me."

"What!?" was my first reaction. I could not believe what I was hearing. How could I go to Europe? That was not the answer I expected Him to bring. I laughed because it was so absurd. Only a crazy person could believe such nonsense. *How can God call a single African girl to Europe!*

It seemed impossible and unrealistic. Even my prayer partners agreed it was absurd when they heard about it. They thought I was going crazy. "God would never send you there!" they reasoned. Indeed, it made no sense.

Sweden was a country I knew nothing about. To my knowledge, I had never met anyone from there. Then I started wondering and questioning God because I thought He was supposed to do things according to our desires and dreams. I knew and believed God worked that way. But why was He sending me there? Sweden was not in my desires or dreams. In fact, I tried to give God some suggestions about where He should send me. I would think, "God, why not send me to countries where I have friends, such as the United States, Great Britain, or Canada?"

I had been to other countries before, so I requested Him to send me back to one of those places: "God, you can send me back to India where I saw so many people worshipping the unknown gods." I gave Him these suggestions because I could not understand why He would send me to a place I could hardly locate on the map! He did not pay any attention to my suggestions. To Him, there is no such thing as "hard" or "impossible." He is a God of "now," dealing with a human being whose tendency is to see impossibilities more clearly than possibilities.

As I tried to find a way out, I realized God meant business. The words He spoke to me, "Go to Sweden and witness for me," could not be ignored.

"The earth is the Lord's and everything in it, the world, and all who live in it." (Psalm 24:1)

Sweden was His, Tanzania was His, and all of us around the globe are His. As I left everything to Him, He started giving me further instructions. One night as I was sleeping, He said, "Nicku, leave Tanzania July 22, 1977." Out of unbelief, I said, "That is too soon!" When God told me something in the past, I would obey without hesitation. I was willing to obey whatever He wanted me to do.

However, I had more doubt than faith in this situation. I could not make any decisions because so many thoughts kept running through my mind.

If you are an African, or if you have lived in Africa, you can understand why I felt that way. *How could I go so far away by myself as an African missionary? Why Europe? Europe is where missionaries are supposed to come from. God, why not send me to other parts of Africa?* I tried to question, to reason, and sometimes felt as if God forgot what He said.

Doubt consumed me. I would have questions or thoughts running in my mind over and over again. *Sweden? Be realistic, I cannot go there,* I would tell myself. But God never gave me an explanation. Indeed, *"God's thoughts are not our thoughts, neither are our ways His ways. His ways are beyond our knowledge. "* (Isaiah 55:9)

In my spirit, I knew He wanted me to go. But as a human being, I was frustrated. It was impossible financially, logically, culturally, and in so many other ways. It was unheard of, at least back home. God did not call a young girl for an overseas mission—did He? Many times when God tells us to do something, we try to use logic because God does not make sense. We think we know better than He does:

"Where is the wise man? Where is the scholar? Where is the philosopher of this age? Has not God made foolish the wisdom of the world? For since in the wisdom of God the world through its wisdom did not know Him, God was pleased through the foolishness of what was preached to save those who believe…For the foolishness of God is wiser than man's wisdom, and the weakness of God is stronger than man's strength." (1 Corinthians 1:20-21, 25)

We reason and argue with Him, forgetting that faith and obedience are required to walk with God. Christians, especially those who have surrendered to the Lordship of Jesus Christ completely, are required to live by faith, not by sight, feelings, or logic.

After I had exhausted all human reasoning and God remained unchanged, I finally accepted the reality of God's unchanging will in this matter and that He fully expected me to obey Him.

Instead of using logic, I should have used faith and embraced the revelation that God was giving me, but I did not. The Bible says,

"God is not a man, that he should lie, nor a son of man that he should change his mind...." (Numbers 23:19)

When the task seems impossible, we want God to change His mind. Nevertheless, after coming to my senses and realizing that God is God, I had no other choice, even if I did not understand it all. I had to lay all human reasoning aside and trust Him.

"We live by faith, not by sight." (2 Corinthians 5:7)

As I started preparing for the trip, I kept the departure date He gave me. Many people thought I was crazy, and some went so far as to think that I was possessed. How could I be so dumb to leave a good job, my car, a three-bedroom house near the beach, and the drive-in cinema merely because "God is calling me to go far away." It would have been OK if I told them, "I have a scholarship to go overseas" or that "a church is sending me there." It would have even made sense if I was preparing to go because some other organization was behind the trip.

If any of the above reasons for leaving Tanzania were true, people would have rejoiced with me and counted me fortunate. Farewell parties would have been prepared. Some would have wanted my contact address. But to say God was the only one sending me to Sweden—that was crazy and unheard of! No one wanted to believe me or support the idea.

"The man without the Spirit does not accept the things that come from the Spirit of God, for they are foolishness to him, and he cannot understand them, because they are spiritually discerned." (1 Corinthians 2:14)

During that time, I discovered that I could not share spiritual things freely with everyone. There are many good Christians who are not familiar with God's ways, and they cannot comprehend some of the revelations God gives to His children.

Those who tried to stop me were genuine Christians. They were concerned about my well-being and did not want to see me leave everything without knowing where in Sweden I was going. As human beings, we have to know!

"Because the foolishness of God is wiser than men; and the weakness of God is stronger than men." (1 Corinthians 1:25)

I had to rely on what seemed like "God's foolishness."

Since I was hearing more negativity than encouragement, I avoided talking about God's call for my life. When people asked about my travel plans, I would not tell the exact truth. I would tell some people I was invited to go preach in Sweden and that was the reason I was making the trip. Since they knew I traveled a lot to preach, they understood. What the word of God says in Romans 8:5 became clearer, *"Those who live according to the sinful nature have their minds set on what that nature desires; but those who live in accordance with the Spirit have their minds set on what the Spirit desires."*

Some of my friends and leaders in the churches would speak in theological terms to convince me to listen to their advice. "Nicku, God uses people. Let us know who is really sending you to Sweden." I did not have the answer they wanted. They did not want to accept what I knew. It was very frustrating at times to know that God did not provide me with all the answers, yet I had to hold fast to His Word and His call.

"The sovereign Lord has opened my ears, and I have not been rebellious, I have not drawn back ... Because the sovereign Lord helps me...." (Isaiah 50:5-7)

I remembered how my father used to say over and over that God does not always tell us everything at once. I grew up knowing what it meant to trust and obey God. I did not have to have all the answers for their questions nor did I have to listen to any negative advice.

Nevertheless, at times I did not always remember Dad's advice and I wavered in my decision. I tried every means available to dismiss the call. I finally yielded to God completely and as soon as I did that, faith was activated. Then I began to understand God's plans more clearly and His provisions began to unfold.

Two weeks before my departure from Dar es Salaam, I was talking with a family friend. When he heard that I had less than fourteen days before I was to leave, he cut me short before I could finish. I did not even have to tell him the whole story. As soon as he heard "Sweden," he started telling me about a lady he knew in Bollnas. He gave me her address and telephone number so I could contact her, convey greetings from his family, or visit her when I got the chance. What he did not realize was that he was being used by God to give me the address. That was the first contact I was given.

I thanked God because He started showing me how He would provide instructions one day at a time as long as I was willing to obey. That family friend did not know anything about my accommodations in Sweden and how the trip came to be. He thought I had been invited and everything was arranged for me.

Before I left Tanzania, however, I asked God to allow me to make two stops en route to Sweden. I wanted to stop in Nairobi, Kenya, and in Milan, Italy. Without having fasted or prayed about it, God gave me approval with specific travel instructions to both places, including what day to leave.

I left Dar es Salaam on July 22, 1977, without purchasing the complete ticket I needed to get me to the mission in Sweden. The money I had was enough to reach Milan. I felt I had to go in obedience to God's leading even if the money for the tickets was not enough and other preparations were not ready. In my spirit, I knew God was in charge, not me or anyone else. I had to take the first step of faith and follow the dates He had made for me. The rest was His business. Money or no money, I left my country.

Although I was unsure, I thought God would use my sister in Italy to buy me the rest of the ticket from Milan to Stockholm. I did not know God had other plans. He used people in Nairobi to give me the rest of the money instead.

When I arrived in Nairobi, Kenya, I went to say goodbye to my friends and the pastor of the church where I was one of the pioneers. The transit was for three days. One day before I left Nairobi, a miracle happened. I was given an envelope that contained some money. It was the exact amount of money I needed to buy the ticket to Stockholm!

It was a miracle because no one knew that my ticket was not purchased in full. No one could have told them. I was in a different country where they wouldn't have heard the rumors claiming "I was crazy." Many questions people asked me back home could not be answered. "How could

I leave everything in Dar es Salaam because God had said so? Was I insane?" I knew they did not hear God's words but man's. When I saw the money, I praised God. He was at work on my behalf.

When God does things, He does them well. He knows all your needs and your thoughts. No one in Nairobi knew I needed money or how much was needed for the remaining portion of the ticket. Only God, my Jehovah-Jireh, knew. When the people handed me the money they said, "Nicku, we want to be a blessing. Take this pocket money for your mission trip." As I thanked God, the story of Abraham's call came to mind,

"Leave your country, your people and
your father's household and go to the land
I will show you." (Genesis 12:1)

Friend, when nobody seems to know what you are going through, do not be discouraged. Remember that there is one who knows all your trials, difficulties, pains, sorrows, and uncertainties. He even knows about those tears that flow from your eyes when no one is around. Even if your friends know what you are going through but don't understand or care, know that God understands and cares.

"Cast all your anxiety on Him because
He cares for you." (1 Peter 5:6)

God did it for me and He has done it over and over as I step out in faith and obedience to His will. He will come through for you in any situation.

Although I had confidence in my sister, God knew how she would react on hearing that I had left everything to answer God's call to "Go." As a human being, I did not know that my "faith walk" was going to upset her, but God knew. All my life, I knew my sister loved me so much that she would do anything I requested, even buying an airline ticket. She was a giving person; it was her nature, and I had no reason to think otherwise, especially knowing the trip was intended to reach the lost souls with the love of Christ.

However, when I arrived in Milan, my sister wasn't herself. She acted indifferent. She wasn't even excited to see me. It did not take long for me to discover the problem. As we talked, it became clear she was very disappointed with my decision. She kept asking why I was going to Sweden. Despite my explanations, she did not understand. She did not believe it was that simple and assumed I had a hidden agenda.

"How can you be so stupid to leave your good job and give away everything just to travel to a strange country believing God wants you there?" she asked. "Nicku, who do you think you are? Have you heard of anyone from Africa being sent to Europe as a missionary without any support or a sponsor? You must be out of your mind."

It was very painful to see my sister so angry! She was concerned with her young sister, who she thought was ignorant of the real world. She was right, though. I did not know much, except that I knew I had heard from God. With that realization, I knew no one could make me think otherwise.

God spoke to me. I then had to choose whether to listen to Him or chose the world's many voices. My sister tried to convince me to remain in Milan with her in case I was tired of living in Tanzania. I refused and again explained why I did not want to stay. Her concern was sincere, but she did not understand that I had a mandate to fulfill. I had a mission in my heart that no one else understood.

In reality, it did not make sense to me either. But I had to obey and trust that God knew best. I was following Jesus, and even if my family could not understand or might disown me, I would still follow Him and all the ways in which He instructed me. Indeed, salvation is free but not cheap. When one answers, "Yes," to God's will, call, or vision, it is usually a "Yes" to obedience, not his or her ability to do the job.

My sister's concern was valid. I did not know anyone in Sweden, nor did I know where I was going to start witnessing. In a world where technology is readily available, planning is easy and expected and, in her eyes, I needed to face the reality of our century. At that time, I was living an illusion and my trip was unrealistic. My sister just could not understand! Telling her about the address and the telephone number I was given did not help either. She thought I was crazy to assume having the name of someone who knew nothing about me was a sign of confirmation that God was leading me. It did not make sense to her. We could not agree with each other on anything.

Culturally, it was considered wrong and impolite to ignore the advice of an elder sister. When any older person gives advice or discipline, the younger is expected to receive it. In my family, I was brought up to respect the elders. I lived life respecting others and following the cultural and moral traditions. Concerning spiritual matters, however, God is always supreme. This was the first time I completely disagreed with my sister, and that was hard for both of us.

The evening before my departure, I asked politely if I could use the telephone to call Sweden. "I hope you are not embarrassing yourself," she replied after agreeing. I did not say a word. I telephoned the lady in Bollnas, introduced myself, and asked if she could meet me at the airport the following evening. She refused out right, stating that it was an imposition for her to drive the 50 miles to the airport—it was just too far! She said many things and even talked about the family that gave me her name in Africa.

I understood why she was reluctant to extend herself on such a short notice, but to say 50 miles was too far for a drive to the airport did not make sense to me.

When my sister learned she refused, she was furious with me. She tried to convince me that God was not sending me there; otherwise, she said, the lady would not have refused to help me.

"How can you just go?" she asked over and over again. "Nicku, stop this foolishness. If you leave, I will disown you as my sister."

Those words pierced my soul; nonetheless, I did not compromise. I knew she was only scared for me. I told her it was OK and that I was leaving the next day as planned because God gave me the date when I was to leave Italy. That I had no place to go nor anyone to meet me did not matter. God would lead me one step at a time.

As I left, my sister cried, refusing even to take me to the airport. My brother-in-law drove me, and we did not speak to each other. I was crying too, because I loved my sister very much, and I did not want to hurt her by disobeying her requests; but there was nothing I could do. I had to leave Milan, even if I was scared myself. I knew God was in control, but I was still afraid, not knowing what I would face in a foreign country. I kept doubting my decision. *If it was God who used my friend to give me the lady's address, then why was she refusing to pick me up?* I asked myself.

The natural man did not have the answer. Thankfully, the spirit within me was strong; I had tasted God's miracles and faithfulness and could not turn back.

"I am with you and will watch over you wherever you go, and I will bring you back to this land. I will not leave you until I have done what I have promised you." (Genesis 28:15)

On the plane, I continued to pray all kinds of prayers. Some were faithless prayers with words of doubt, fear, and complaints. I asked God not to let me down; otherwise, it would be to His shame. People at home would blame Him if He did not take care of a girl who trusted Him wholeheartedly. As we flew through the blue sky, a million thoughts flashed through my mind. *What will I say when I land in Stockholm? Where will I say I am going if I am asked by the immigration? Who will help me to find my first transportation in a foreign land?* I do not remember anything from that flight. I was too engrossed in my thoughts and trying to commune with my Lord. He had to speak before the plane landed in Stockholm, Sweden.

As we were about to land for a stopover in Copenhagen, Denmark, the Holy Spirit urged me to look toward the front of the airplane. At first it felt strange. *What was I supposed to be looking for?* I kept my eyes wide open, staring, but not looking. Suddenly, the Holy Spirit pointed out one person to whom I should talk. She was five rows in front of me. I felt like going to talk to her immediately, but the Spirit told me to wait and hold my peace. It was hard because I did not want her to disappear.

The plane landed and the transit passengers were told to go in the transit lounge. I thought I would rush from my seat to catch her, but it was impossible to jump over to the aisle from my window seat. The aisles were crowded with those who wanted to connect with other flights. I knew I had lost her. As we disembarked, I kept on looking around. Fortunately, I saw her seated alone in the transit lounge, seemingly waiting on someone.

I went over and started a conversation by complimenting her on the outfit she was wearing. After exchanging greetings and my reason for the trip, I told her I was going to Bollnas and did not know how much the taxi from Stockholm would cost. "I would appreciate it if you would give me an idea," I inquired. She looked at me and said, "Taxi to Bollnas! Are you very rich?" I smiled, but I did not know why she sounded so shocked.

As we continued to talk, I was surprised no taxi traveled that far. *But how far was 50 miles?* Thankfully, she was going farther than I. Her car was at the Arlanda Airport (in Stockholm), and she was driving north to Sundsvall, north of Bollnas. She offered me a ride to Bollnas. Indeed, God was directing! I had talked to the right person. I jumped at the offer to ride with her.

When we returned to the plane, I thanked God with tears of joy flowing down my cheeks. Imagine if I had been too shy to talk to her. I would have missed God's plan for me. Above all, I believe God had prepared her to help me. He was faithful to lead me one step at a time as long as I was in tune with Him, listening to the inner voice within me.

*"A man's steps are directed by the
Lord...."* (Proverbs 20:24)

When we came to Arlanda Airport outside Stockholm, she took my passport and gave it to the Immigration officers. I did not hear what she said, and they did not ask me any questions as they stamped my passport. We got through customs, and I was following her out when someone from behind us called my name. "Nicku." I was in shock. *Who could be calling my name in a strange country?*

I turned to look and did not see anyone who could know me. I thought maybe if I saw an African, then I could assume the person might know or had seen me from somewhere, but there was no African around.

As I turned to continue walking, again a voice shouted, "Nicku." I stopped and looked in the direction from which the voice came. An elderly lady came and embraced me. "Here you are! Welcome to Sweden," she said. She was speaking in our national language, Swahili. That shocked me even more, so I asked who she was.

"I am Ruth," she replied, "the lady whom you talked with on the phone when you called from Italy." With bright eyes, I asked, "How come you are here? Why do you speak

Swahili and not English?" (At that time, I still did not know that in Sweden they spoke Swedish, not English!)

The other lady I met on the transit stood for a while then left us. In shock, I did not know what to do except ask questions. "But Ruth, yesterday you told me you would not come to meet me!" She answered and said, "Last night I could not sleep. The Holy Spirit spoke to me very strongly that I must come meet you."

Although I could not understand her Swahili very well, I was impressed.

"I had to call a friend to drive me here," she said. "That is why I came. God wants me to take you to my home."

I did not have anything more to say except to praise God for His care. He provided two people. The lady I met in the plane helped me get through the immigration because they did not ask any questions. They only provided my passport. What she said to them I do not know. At the same time, I felt there was no problem because God was in control of every step I took.

God then brought Ruth to provide transportation and accommodation until I heard further instruction from Him.

"... A man plans his course, but the Lord determines his steps." (Proverbs 16:9)

We left Arlanda Airport and drove more than six hours to reach Bollnas, where Ruth lived. It was then that I understood Swedish mileage was different from British mileage. When she said Bollnas was 50 miles away, she meant it was about 500 kilometers—the equivalent of 310 miles. One Swedish mile is about ten kilometers.

The trip was long, especially since it was in the evening and I was with two strangers (Ruth and the friend who drove her to the airport) who did not understand me nor God's vision and mission.

As she asked strange questions in her broken Swahili, I did not know what to expect or where I was being taken. Thoughts of fear and uncertainty kept flashing in my mind. I felt like the whole world was laughing at my stupid trip. Physically, I was tired, but my mind could not rest. The devil had finally succeeded in getting a loophole. He kept saying, *"Who do you think you are to come to Europe? Who will support you? Even Ruth is doubting whether God really called you here!"* My mind was my own enemy.

Somehow, though, I heard the still, small voice encouraging me to trust God, to count on the miracles that had already occurred since the mission trip started. As I got my mind off of the devil's lies and focused on God's promises, I remembered that He was in control.

Chapter 7

"Lord, Why Am I Here?"

On the first day, my host tried to teach me how to use her toilet. Many things she said indicated that she thought I was a very primitive African. It did not bother me. I gave her the benefit of the doubt because she had lived in some remote African villages in the 1940's and 1950's.

However, after two days of living with Ruth, I started to feel that I was in the wrong place. At times it was annoying to be told I should be careful handling the dishes or not to use glasses because I might break them. There was an obvious assumption that this was my first time seeing pretty dishes. Our communication was a struggle, and I was regarded as a "bush girl." Ruth tried to explain everything, including how to use a teacup. It was embarrassing, and I started questioning God.

How could He send me to a country where I did not speak the language!? Above all, how could I live with a lady who did not think I was capable of communicating apart from my African language? Until I arrived, I did not know that Sweden had its own language.

Back home in Tanzania most of us thought that all Europeans spoke English.

So by answering God's call I thought I could just stand and witness about God's love in Bollnas using English without any problems. To talk with people was hard for me, but now I had no means to even start a conversation. The language was a barrier. It was a very frustrating situation..

To make matters worse, my host, Ruth, did not speak English; we communicated using Swahili, the national language of Tanzania and other East African countries. Ruth learned Swahili in the '40s when she was a missionary in Congo (now Zaire). Her Swahili was very broken and rusty. When she spoke, I had to listen carefully. Even then, I only managed to understand a little, but I doubt if she understood me at all! Her facial and body language showed disgust, as if I knew nothing. It was a challenge. I could not figure out why I was there! If God sent me, He should have prepared someone or some place where language was not a problem.

When we went to church the first Sunday morning, I was looking forward to praising God. To my surprise, I could not understand a thing! Their songs sounded dull. There was no melody that I recognized. Inside the church, I felt lost and lonely. After the service, people started talking and shaking each other's hands, but, to my shock, nobody came to say hello to me. Some even came very near and talked with Ruth. After they were through, they greeted one another and passed me by as if I did not exist. We stood there for twenty minutes, and I felt like I was just a statue from Africa.

Standing outside the church like an invisible person shocked me. It brought doubt even to my calling to Sweden. *Had I really heard from God? Why was it that nothing seemed to indicate God's love? How could God send me to these unfriendly people?* I started to feel very homesick, missing my home and my churches. I could not comprehend the cultural difference! *Has God really created us all to be so different?*

People in Tanzania, especially my hometown, were more hospitable to strangers. Our churches are very friendly to everybody. In fact, it is an African cultural strength to be sociable to visitors and strangers. I thought of my parents and how they loved visitors. The more I thought about my culture, the more difficult it was to understand why no one talked to me.

Instead of being uplifted, I cried endlessly. I told God that my being there was a mistake, and that I could not stay any longer. I even confessed that maybe had I not heard Him properly and that He should forgive me. I thought that Sweden was not where He wanted me to be.

I went on and on crying and confessing until that evening. No answer came directly from above and that frustrated me even more. I was desperate to hear from Him.

After I stopped crying and questioning God without any response, I told Ruth I was going back to Tanzania. Apologetically, I confessed that it was a mistake to have come to Sweden. I must not have heard from God because it was difficult for me to witness anywhere since I did not speak Swedish. To continue my stay would be a waste of time.

Ruth continued what she was doing without paying any attention to what I was saying. I went back to my room and fell on my knees to pray. I doubt whether I spoke or meditated my prayer, but I know I buried my face in my hands and pressed it on the bed as tears rolled down my cheeks. I kept questioning God until I fell asleep while still on my knees. When I got up, my body was very tired. It felt like I had been hit by a truck!

The next day—Monday morning—a telephone call came. Ruth spoke with the person for a while and then called me. I went to see her, and she gave me the phone angrily. She began to instruct me on how to talk on the phone and where to hold the receiver. It was obvious she thought I had never used a phone before. Evidently, she had even forgotten that I called her from Italy! She continued to act like I was from the dark ages. I did not blame her. She was an old lady who thought I came from the bush of Africa. I knew God had a purpose for everything.

I took the phone without knowing who was calling me and wondered why Ruth seemed so angry when she handed me the receiver.

"Hallow," I said, anticipating the upcoming conversation. The person on the line asked if I understood English, and I told her that I did. It was refreshing to hear someone talk to me in a language I could understand. The person on the other end was shocked to hear that I spoke English. I could tell she was relieved. She then asked me why and how I had come to Sweden. I gave her brief information, mixed with logic, about my mission calling.

"After being in Bollnas three days," I went on to tell her, "I realize I have made a mistake, and I am ready to go home as soon as I can get a train to Stockholm." After talking for a while, she was sympathetic because she had heard a different story from Ruth. She told me not to waste any money to take a train. She would make arrangements with someone to drive me back to Stockholm. I was pleased to talk with her. Ruth stood there wondering what we were talking about. I told her as much as I could.

The same lady called back the following day and told me that an African girl was going to be picking me up. She said the girl used to live there before she moved to Vasteras (a city near Stockholm). She would be there on Sunday and then drive me to the airport in Stockholm.

"As I spoke with her," the woman added, "I was amazed because she felt she was going to drive to Bollnas very soon. This girl was being prepared to travel even before we knew it." She then concluded, "God is on your side." I thanked her, put down the receiver, and went to pray.

I did not want to be there. I wanted to leave for home immediately. But somehow, I agreed to stay six more days. Those were the longest six days I ever experienced. It was like a force pushed me to agree with her. "Wait for a ride!" This African girl was going to drive over 600 kilometers to pick me up! That must have been God, but I did not think that way then. I cried most of the time and missed my people in Africa. I also was very uncomfortable with my host. I often wished God would speed up the clock!

On Thursday, someone called to inform Ruth that there was going to be a tent meeting on Saturday somewhere outside Bollnas. She invited Ruth to come. When she came on Saturday to pick Ruth up, I went along. It was a thrill to get out of the house, and I thanked her in English for coming. She was shocked to hear me speak English, but I could not understand why.

Later, I discovered that Ruth had been telling people who inquired about me that I was crazy to think I would evangelize Sweden by speaking Swahili. The lady who was driving knew some English, and she narrated what she heard from Ruth and others. We talked and laughed about it. She was very exuberant and said, "You see, age can make you change stories about others."

It was the first time since I arrived that I found someone so nice and friendly. Her sense of humor put me at ease.

The trip to the meeting was pleasant; it helped me laugh off some of my frustrations.

As we approached the tent, we could hear familiar songs of praise and worship. I wanted to rush in! As we took our seats, I felt God's presence and had peace in my spirit. I suddenly felt at home among strangers in a strange land. It was nice to lift my hands and worship Him. I recognized the melody of some of the songs, so I sang along in my language or in English. Although I had my eyes closed, I was not concentrating on Him completely. My worship was a mixture of praises and complaints. As I sang in my language, I visualized my people and wanted to be there with them. Nevertheless, I thanked God for who He was, yet still complained about why He had sent me so far and made me look like a fool.

As I was engrossed in my spiritual world, a very big man came over to me, tapped me on the shoulder, and asked, "Miss, how long are you going to be here?" I told him I was leaving the next day for Vasteras and then going to Tanzania. He protested and said, "No! As soon as I saw you, God told me you should come to the Bible school."

He gave me a card and said, "Here is my contact." In my mind, I dismissed it as nonsense because I did not want to hear it. After all, I was there only because I was waiting for a ride to take me to Stockholm. My mind was made up to go back home. I had concluded that being in Sweden was a big mistake and no one could say otherwise. While the kind man was talking, I almost blocked my ears and did not want to hear, especially when he said, "God told me." I felt like telling him, "Sir, do not tell me about what God told you because God told me to leave my people and all I had and come here."

Tears almost ran down my cheeks as I thought about all the things I would like to tell him: "Look, now I am regarded as a bush girl who does not know anything. Besides, I cannot even go out to witness because I do not know the language. What kind of mission is this? Just leave me alone."

I am glad I did not verbalize those words to him, but I wonder how he perceived my facial expression. However, before he went back to his seat, he reminded me to use his calling card that had the school's address and said, "Please call me when you are ready." Since it was still in my hand, I looked at it but as soon as he turned to go, I threw it down on the grass where we were sitting. After the meeting, we left and the card remained inside the tent. I had forgotten what Jesus said in Mark 10:29-30:

" 'I tell you the truth,' Jesus replied, 'no one who has left home or brothers or sisters or mother or father or children or fields for me and the gospel will fail to receive a hundred times as much in this present age (homes, brothers, sisters, mothers, children and fields- and with them, persecutions) and in the age to come, eternal life.' "

On Sunday morning, I was not looking forward to going to church. I was looking forward to leaving. As promised, the girl came to pick me up. What a relief! I was ready to leave, but I was not sure if she needed to rest first. Inside me, I wished we would leave immediately. God answered my desires. She told me to take my things to the car. She did not even want to talk long with my host. She wanted to avoid any idle word that Ruth might say. We left Bollnas for the airport about 600 kilometers away via Vasteras. In the car, we talked about Africa, my experiences there, etc. The five-hour drive did not seem long at all. She was friendly and sympathetic to my situation. She also knew Ruth very well.

It became evident that we could not go directly to the airport since it was night and there were no more flights to Tanzania that day. She asked me to stay with her for a few days so that I could tell her more about Jesus. During our conversation, I could sense she had been hurt. Although she offered to have me stay with her, I did not want to but inside my spirit, I prayed, *"God, if you sent me all the way from Africa to come to Sweden for the purpose of this one girl, I will be happy if she falls in love with you."* Without thinking it through, I agreed to stay with her for a few days. We both laughed and reached her place in a joyous mood.

Her house was filled with liquor, posters of rock stars, and music records. I was not surprised. Immediately, I went into the bathroom and prayed. I consecrated the house and everything in it. I knew God had a purpose for putting me there.

"Whatever town or village you enter, search for some worthy person there and stay at his house until you leave ... He who receives you receives me, and he who receives me receives the one who sent me. Anyone who receives a prophet because he is a prophet will receive a prophet's reward, and anyone who receives a righteous man because he is a righteous man will receive a righteous man's reward. And if anyone gives even a cup of cold water to one of these little ones because he is my disciple, I tell you the truth, he will certainly not lose his reward." (Matthew 10:11, 40-42)

I started telling her about salvation and the abundant life to be found in Christ and that the life she was living outside of Jesus was death and not worth it. The first day she was polite and did not say much. Then she became honest with me.

"Nicku," she said, "when I came from Africa, I was a Christian and my father was a preacher." She went on, "I am disappointed with Christians here. It is not like back home. The missionary lady who brought me here from home mistreated me. She wanted me to be her servant."

She turned her face away to look out the window. "When I tried to go to some churches," she went on to say, "I could not find anybody who cared about me. Out of desperation, I started looking for people who would accept me." She looked back at me, and I noticed tears rolling down her cheeks. "Now I enjoy life in discotheques and night clubs. These people love me, and they know my name. Therefore, do not tell me about God's love and Christianity anymore."

She walked into the kitchen, and for a moment I did not say a word. I felt so sad for her and started to pray with agony. At the same time, I knew exactly what she was talking about.

Yet, as much as I understood what she was saying, I did not let her experience hinder me from sharing the reality of God's love. God was teaching us to look to Him and not men, for they are bound to disappoint us. God confirmed this when Jesus was transfigured. He told Peter, "This is my son, … listen to him" (Matthew 17:4-5). I referred to several scriptures concerning God's love demonstrated through Christ. I wanted her to try to embrace Jesus, not people. Jesus is our example. He is a true friend who saves us out of sin and religion. Jesus puts us in fellowship and relationship with Him.

I had two more days to stay with her before my departure for Africa. I continued to say to her, "You should not look to people but rather look to Jesus. People will fail you, but God will never let you down." At this time, I was consumed with trying to lead her to Christ. I fasted and prayed endlessly. My spirit was vexed because of the lifestyle that she had adopted. Her bad experiences with some Christians made her bitter. No matter what I said, she did not want to believe it. Her mind was made up; although, her spirit could testify that "Jesus is the way, the truth and the life."

One day before my departure, I was having my devotions when God spoke to me through Joshua 1:8-9. It says:

"Do not let this Book of the Law depart from your mouth; meditate on it day and night, so that you may be careful to do everything written in it. Then you will be prosperous and successful. Have I not commanded you? Be strong and courageous. Do not be terrified; do not be discouraged, for the Lord your God will be with you wherever you go."

I read the scriptures over and over. They did not have any special impact. I closed my Bible and knelt beside the bed. As I meditated, God told me not to leave without accomplishing what He had sent me to do. I almost laughed. Throughout the day, the thought kept coming to me, but I did not want to hear it.

That night, I could not sleep; I kept on tossing. I got off my bed and started praying. I walked around the room wondering what God wanted me to do. Finally, I said, "Lord, reveal to me your will. Let me understand."

It was like telling God to speak to me in plain language. I did not know what God was talking about when he said,

"Do not leave without accomplishing the mission," nor what He wanted me to do! *Was He referring to the mission in Sweden or to the girl?* As far as I was concerned, I felt I had done my part.

When morning came, I decided to continue to tell her about God's love, hoping she would receive Christ as Lord and Savior so my mission could be complete before I left. However, I did not know that she was annoyed with my faith-based lifestyle. As I started sharing, she said, "Nicku, I do not want you to keep on praying and fasting in my home." She stood up and continued, "Since you have been here, I cannot bring friends over. I told you; I do not want to sleep alone, and I do not want to be saved."

While she spoke, she walked a few steps to the bookshelf and picked up something. She turned toward me and handed me a paper. "I was given this two years ago when some other people came to witness in my house," she said. She pointed toward the cabinets and continued, "They condemned me for all these bottles of alcohol that I have used as decoration. They told me when they came again that I should have thrown them all away, but I told them never to come back again and they did not." By this time, she was very angry and could not sit still. She kept pacing back and forth.

As I looked at the paper, she went on, "One thing that I cannot understand is you. You are an African girl telling me the same thing as the people who gave me that paper!"

I looked at the paper she had given me and saw that it was a tract written in Swedish.

"Why are you giving me a Swedish tract?" I asked. Sarcastically, she answered, "To let you know that I have Christian literature in the house, and since your God can reveal anything to you, I am sure you can read that tract even if it is in a language you do not know." I was dumbfounded and did not say anything more to her. She walked to the kitchen to get something to drink.

As I was gazing at the tract in my hand, the Spirit within me said, "Turn it over to the other side." When I turned it over, I could not believe it! On that paper was the same address that I was given in Bollnas by the huge man at the tent meeting. As I stared at it, the Spirit again said, "Your mission is not over." Immediately, I knew God wanted me to go to the school as a place of contact for my mission. But I struggled within my soul, and I did not want to obey. I wanted to be in Africa.

The harder I tried to ignore God's Spirit talking to me, the louder I felt Him speak. Out of curiosity, I decided to try the Spirit. I called the number on the tract. As soon as I told her who I was, the woman on the other end replied, "Where have you been? Since he gave you the calling card, he has been talking about expecting your call." She put me on hold, wanting to clarify something, then she came on and said, "Where are you and when are you coming up?"

I could not believe what I was hearing. She talked with me as if we knew each other. I almost confessed that

I threw his card away, but I was embarrassed to tell the truth. All her questions during our conversation came as a surprise; I thought the people at the school would not recall anything about me. The man who gave me his card spoke with me less than a minute at the tent meeting! God's ways are not our ways. He always confirms His word with signs and wonders.

Instead of being taken to the airport, I went to catch a train to go to Bethel Institute in Orissa. It was close to Bollnas, where God took me initially. I later discovered that the man who had given me the address was the principal and founder of the Bible school, Mr. Ebbe Bollin.

I started attending some of the classes just to hear what they were teaching and how Swedish sounded. It was hard to concentrate. Even if a person tried to translate the lecture for me, after twenty minutes, I would lose concentration and could not understand a thing.

As I began to know people, I realized that spiritual awakening was higher in Africa than in European countries. At home, because people take God's word in faith and with simplicity, many get saved. Miracles are taken as part of God's promise to His children.

I was impressed, however, because at this school the students were being trained to follow God and to walk by faith. It was not theory alone but practical experience to believe in God's Word and to fulfill the Great Commission at all cost. Although my desire to go back home was still very strong, God revealed to many people, including the school principal and myself, that my mission in Sweden was for His glory. His purpose for sending me to be a missionary/evangelist in Sweden would be revealed as I continued to obey and serve Him.

It was during that year, between September 1977 and May 1978, that I traveled around Sweden, Finland, and Norway to share about the power of Jesus. I still could not speak Swedish, but God provided different students to be my interpreters. Sometimes, if the students could not go with me, I would go to churches where there was someone to interpret.

I recall helping several students in their walk with God. One girl thought sex before marriage was acceptable because they both were in the Bible School and she intended to get married. I counseled her for a while, and she was delivered from immorality. Her boyfriend decided to leave her, but the girl stood in her decision to live for Christ.

After spending time with the boy, showing him what the Bible says, he repented. Several girls confessed doing the same thing because the culture did not condemn this. I told them God will judge us according to His word and nothing else.

God's hand was in every meeting at school or in our rooms. When I went evangelizing, people received Christ as their personal Savior for the first time; others were healed and filled with the Holy Spirit. One evening, I preached in a church nearby and six people received Christ. A man in his seventies told my interpreter, "This foreign Jesus is more powerful than ours." Some experienced firsthand the miracle of what it means to walk by faith. My testimony about how God led me to Sweden encouraged them. They experienced the reality of Philip and the Ethiopian eunuch (Acts 8:26). Many called me a missionary from Africa because I was not disobedient to the vision that God showed me at a very early age.

I believe there is much to learn from all cultures. I saw that the Scandinavian Christians needed to hear and see the faith of the African Christians. I praise God because He used an ordinary girl to proclaim His word. The word did not return void. He saved and healed many who were afflicted. One man could not use his hand; when I prayed for him, his fingers became straight instantly.

Another was blind for years, but God restored his sight. One family lived in constant conflict. I counseled them for an hour; we prayed, and they were transformed. God restored love and tranquility. All glory belongs to God!

I thanked God for being at Bethel. I felt I was accomplishing the mission He had given me—"Go and serve me far away." I did that, and I was ready to return home. I prayed and begged earnestly for God to take me back to Tanzania.

"Lord, I have accomplished your mission. I want to return home. Please take me to my people." That was my prayer. I talked and dreamed about going home. Everyone around me, however, seemed to have a different opinion.

Chapter 8

Dr. Yonggi Cho in Stockholm

In May 1978, the principal and students of Bethel Bible School who spoke English were selected to go to Stockholm for the Yonggi Cho Conference, held in Folket Hus. The principal wanted me to go specifically so I could worship and enjoy ministry in English. For months I had not heard any English preaching except for my own.

Stockholm was thrilling. I was in Sweden for nine months and still had never made it to the capital city, except when I first arrived at the airport.

When we arrived for the conference, I thought about going somewhere to witness. As I prayed about it, I felt the best place to start was with the foreign missions.

I took one of my friends, and we went to the Tanzanian Embassy. It was exciting because there were people from home that I could talk to in our national language. It was also an opportunity to invite others to attend the conference.

When we arrived at the embassy, they extended the Tanzanian courtesy. I talked in Swahili endlessly, while my Norwegian friend looked through the newspaper. I told the officers why I was in Sweden and why I was in Stockholm: "To attend Yonggi Cho's Conference and witness in the streets about God's love."

They were astonished! How could it be? A Tanzanian girl saying she is in Northern Europe witnessing for Christ! That was very unusual and sounded very strange. We talked inside the conference room. As we drank "Afri-coffee," they mocked me. Some officers turned to ask my friend if it was true; others seemed a little suspicious of my mission. I did not mind because I knew that the things of God are foolishness to the world. I continued to talk to them about God and invited them to fall in love with Christ. In no uncertain way, I told them that He is the only answer for every problem in their lives and in the world.

We talked for a while longer. One officer went and called others to come and meet us. I was amazed because they did not send me away. Although they thought and said I was crazy, they seemed to enjoy our presence. They were kind and keen to hear more, not about Jesus alone but about me also. Above all, they suggested I should meet the ambassador over lunch. That was God! I was so happy when they requested that my Norwegian friend and I stay. I praised God because it was He who gave us favor and approval. I counted it as another opportunity to shine for Him and share Jesus with the diplomats.

I also wanted to use this opportunity to share my concern with them. I had been telling God all along that before I left for Africa that summer, I wanted to have money to buy offering collection boxes for churches at home. I wanted to take gifts for the churches. When I saw the silver collection boxes in the Swedish churches, I fell in love with them. I thought they would be perfect gifts for my home churches. They were heavy, designed with two handles and a cross on both sides. I wanted God to perform a miracle so I could work, get some money, and buy two boxes for every church at home.

While we sat eating at the table with the embassy officials, we were relaxed and I shared this with them. I mentioned that I would like to have a job for one month before I left the country, so I could buy presents for some churches back home. They all laughed. I could not understand what was so funny.

I shared my concern in sincerity and wanted their help or suggestions, not laughter. "What is wrong?" I asked politely. One officer said, "Don't you think it is funny to talk about presents for churches instead of presents for your family?"

They did not understand that God was first in my life. Although I told them that I left all for the sake of the Gospel, they did not know what that meant. Or at least they thought I was just joking because they had never met a Tanzanian who acted like me.

I had to explain that everything I did was (and is) to serve God and work for Him. I learned to lay my treasures in heaven:

"... Where moth and rust do not destroy, and where thieves do not break in and steal. For where your treasure is, there your heart will be also...." (Matthew 6:20-21)

"How can a young girl waste her life with mission work? You are bright. You can do something better than being religious," the ambassador said. Politely, I replied, "Sir, there is nothing better than what God has called me to do." I went on sharing God's Word. "What good is it for a man to gain the whole world, yet forfeit his soul?" I asked them, quoting Mark 8:36. It was fulfilling to see their attentiveness to everything I shared. I planted God's seed.

After the conference, we returned to Orissa. I received a letter from the Embassy a few days later. I was afraid for a moment of what I might read! Questions came to my mind. *Had I broken any law by witnessing and praying in the Embassy? What had I done to receive a letter just after being there?* Slowly, I opened and read it.

They were having interviews for a secretarial position, and they asked me if I wanted to apply. That was good news. I continued reading with inner gladness. However, they insisted they wanted someone who knew Swedish. By faith, I was happy to take the chance. I told God He had to intervene since I could neither speak nor read Swedish.

The time came for me to go to Stockholm for the interview at the Tanzanian Embassy. As I went to the interview, I made sure God understood why I needed the money—to buy collection boxes for the churches and to get some electric guitars, if I could get enough money.

It is amazing how we try to give God instructions—telling Him our plans as if He does not know and will do them just because we ask. There is a difference between praying and trying to tell Him what to do.

When I arrived at the embassy, there were more than six people seeking the job. Most of them were more qualified than I was, but I did not look at their qualifications or outward appearances; I looked only to my God who knew my intentions. Within my spirit, I communicated with Him. I believed He would do a miracle in spite of myself.

"Trust in the Lord, with all your heart, and lean not on your own understanding. In all your ways acknowledge Him, and He will make your paths straight." (Proverbs 3:5-6)

After the interview, I took the train and went back to Orissa. When my friends asked me how the interview went, I told them confidently, "God is handling my situation. I will get the job."

One friend, Doris, said, "I have no doubt, if you say so." She had grown to love me because God had confirmed several things through me. She also knew my ability to depend on God without reservation and that also made her agree that I would get the job. Others thought I was joking because I did not know Swedish, and the letter said they needed someone who spoke Swedish.

Sure enough, four days later I received a letter telling me to report for work in June. God is above man's regulations. His ways are above ours. We need to trust Him to do more than we can ask or imagine. I knew He wanted me to have some money to buy presents for my African churches, but, more importantly, He wanted me to continue telling the embassy people and others in Stockholm about God's love and His saving grace. God wanted me to be His ambassador in the embassy.

Chapter 9

God's Plans Prevail!

Taking a job in Stockholm required me to have a place to live. I did not know where to live in the Swedish capital, but I knew who to ask. I started praying, "My God, who provided me with a job, is able to provide a place for me to live." Friends tried to offer suggestions. Doris was willing to contact her family, so I could live with them for one month. As I prayed, I was being told to anticipate more. I felt I needed a place of my own, and God was going to do the impossible.

> *"Dear friends, if our hearts do not condemn us, we have confidence before God and receive from him anything we ask, because we obey his commands and do what pleases him."* (1 John 3:21-22)

Not long after, I was reminded of the apartment we stayed at while at the Yonggi Cho Conference. The Spirit told me, "You stayed there, and you will stay there again."

I contacted the owner to see if I could live there. "No, the house is for ministers and missionaries who come to Stockholm from every area of the country," she replied sweetly.

"Sister," I said, "I will be there for one month only; let me use the apartment, and I will take good care of everything."

"Nicku, no," she answered. "There is no week that passes without visitors using the place. You saw the many ministers who used the apartment during the conference."

Indeed, it was a very nice, huge, and self-contained two-room apartment that was well furnished and right in the prestigious area of the City Center. It was a guesthouse for the famous. Although she said no (even the principal of Bethel affirmed that it was impossible to live there), the Spirit within me did not accept it. I knew the God I serve had the final word, so I kept thanking Him for the apartment at Sveavagen 130.

When I saw the owner, I would tell her, "Sister Mailis, I thank God for Sveavagen 130." She would look at me like I was crazy. For two weeks, I kept on saying the same thing. The owner and all the teachers kept saying it was impossible. My friend Doris began to doubt if God would pull through for me. She called her brother and sister, who lived in the suburbs, to see if I could live with them, and they agreed. I told Doris not to worry. Sveavagen 130 was my place.

One day, the owner said, "Nicku, you are wasting your time. You had better be serious about getting accommodations rather than my apartment." I looked at her and smiled. "I am thanking God because He let me stay there during the Conference. I know He had a purpose." I reached for her shoulders and said, "Sister, don't worry about it. I am just praising God for Sveavagen 130." She did not know what to say. She looked at me, shook her head in disbelief, and walked away. I went to my room and praised God for the peace that He had given me in this situation.

"[God] is able to do immeasurably more than all
we ask or imagine, according to his power that
is at work within us...." (Ephesians 3:20)

Indeed, God's Word is true. I had been thinking about the Sveavagen apartment number, 130. God promised and was willing to work above my request, even above the owner's desire. The power in me, or rather the faith in me, kept on praising God over an impossible situation. Is there any impossible situation in your life? If you know that God has spoken to you concerning the matter, don't give up; keep on praising God. There is a reason why He wants you to have something or to do what He is showing you.

Two days before I left, Sister Mailis came to me and said, "Nicku, I don't know why I am doing this, but here is the key for Sveavagen 130." I leaped for joy. Although she did not know the "why," I knew she was obeying God. Slowly, I took the key from her hand and thanked God first, then I hugged and thanked her.

God answered my prayer exceedingly, abundantly, and above all that I asked or thought. When she gave me the key, she said she would not charge me for any rent. I could stay for free and continue to serve God. Indeed, God is faithful!

With that, I moved to Stockholm and started working. The office was not far. After being at the embassy for one month, I started preparing to go home. I knew that my mission was over. I received the wages, purchased my gifts, and looked forward to seeing my people. Many Christians around me, however, did not want to see me go. They kept on saying God still wanted me to serve Him in Sweden. "Please do not say that," I would protest. I was so homesick. I did not want to listen to any more spiritual advice.

At the office too, when I told the ambassador I was leaving, he did not accept it. He said, "We did not employ you for one month only; rather, you can stay as long as you want." I tried to explain that it was my intention from the first day to work only for one month. They told me that they agreed to it because they knew I would stay. I could not believe what I was hearing because the offer was too good to be true. *Why were they saying I would stay?* It sounded fishy. Nonetheless, my desire for Tanzania was greater than my desire to stay in Sweden. My mind was made up to go home. My mission was accomplished.

After I moved into that apartment, I prayed for God to use me to reach people in the streets. I would go out witnessing and invite people from all walks of life to come and taste some African coffee in my house. People would come and then I would tell them about God's love. Some would come specifically for coffee; others to see what kind of a person I was.

The location was ideal for anyone and the atmosphere was pleasant and classy, so people felt special when I invited them there for coffee or tea. I was friendly toward those I approached and showed a genuine interest in wanting to know them. This was part of my strategy to share the Good News with them. Some refused and some accepted the invitation. Oftentimes, I would cook in case some of them wanted to eat.

Several people who came experienced the manifestations of God. One man who was bound by nicotine was set free instantly. An alcoholic woman stayed two days with me and she was set free. Some were healed, countless needs were met, and food was multiplied so I could feed the people who came. Most people who came to the house received something from God in special and unique ways. Let me illustrate how one miracle changed the lives of those who experienced it.

As I had mentioned above, I tried to provide coffee and food to those who came to my apartment. I used to have open house on Saturdays. On this particular Saturday, I did not have much food to prepare or money to buy any. All I had was milk, juice, ice and half a chicken. I looked around, and I saw a bag of all-purpose flour in the cabinet. I praised God and began to cook. I prepared chicken stew and "chapati" (similar to pancakes).

My friend, Nicky, came and we arranged the room for visitors. Food and drinks were put on the kitchen table. Usually anyone who came was sent there to take whatever they needed—it was self-serve. Today was no different. People came and went to the kitchen table and took the chapati and chicken stew. After five people took their meal, I felt something was happening. Some people had a drumstick, while others had different parts of the chicken—thighs, breasts, and wings. I looked and said, "This cannot be!"

I had half a chicken, not enough to feed this many people. I got up and went to the kitchen table to check. The stew was just as I had left it. I called Nicky and showed her what was happening.

"It is a miracle!" she said. "Don't shout. Let us just wait and see!" We went back to join the visitors and shared the Bible.

That day, over twenty people came from the streets, and all of them were able to eat. The chapati and chicken stew continued to multiply. I would look at Nicky throughout the evening and tears of joy would roll down my cheeks. I kept on sending her to the kitchen to look. She and I would whisper, "It is still there!" I thought if I kept going to look, the miracle might stop because my faith was mixed with doubt or uncertainty.

Just before everyone left, we told the people what was going on in our kitchen. They came to see. The food was still there as if no one had eaten anything. We praised God and the miracle became the talk of the town. On Sunday, I went to church and told my pastor and four friends came to see the miracle food after the service. Once again, I served the same dish for our "Sunday Dinner." The following weeks, the group continued to grow. God supplied my needs to help others.

I often wonder why it is so unbelievable when miracles happen. Yet God's Word promises us that,

"No eye has seen, no ear has heard, no mind has conceived what God has prepared for those who love him." (1 Corinthians 2:9)

When I saw the food multiply, I should have just believed! But that was not the case. Time and time again, I have seen God's miracles, yet it takes me a while to praise Him. Our human nature cannot comprehend the supernatural. We need to walk beyond the realm of the natural.

As Christians, we are a peculiar people, and miracles should be a normal way of life for us. A supernatural miracle occurred every month that I was in Sweden, yet I kept on begging God to send me home. My mind did not readily submit to God and say, "God brought me here; therefore, He is in control." No, my mind wanted to be in control.

Although every one around me did not want me to leave, I continued to pack my bags and prepare for the trip home. I was busy praying late one night about what I should preach as my last sermon in Sweden when the telephone rang.

"I am calling from Boras, and I want to talk to you," said the woman on the other end. "I called Orissa, but they said you were no longer there."

She paused before continuing. "I insisted on getting your telephone number because I have a message that you need to hear tonight. Nicku, do not run away from God." When I asked her what she meant, she said, "I do not know, but God forced me to get in touch with you immediately. Do not run away from Him." This message came as a bombshell to me and my spirit.

However, while she was on the phone, I pretended I did not know what she meant. Yet deep inside, I knew what God was telling me. I tried to get her name and telephone number to call her back in the morning. She refused, saying it was not important. "I had a message for you, and I have delivered it. There is no need to call," she concluded.

After I put down the receiver, I fell on my knees and cried bitterly. I vividly remember being on my knees for hours with my face on my bed. I cried until I could not cry anymore. I was angry and frustrated. I could not figure out what God wanted from me. He knew I did not want to be there at all!

When I came to my senses, I calmed down. I talked to God with deep sincerity from my soul. Then I repented, reminding Him I was human and that He should forgive my tears and anger. In honesty, I prayed, *"God, from now on have your own way in my life. I know you know that I love you and that I want to go back to my people, but if you want me in Sweden, or anywhere else, I will stay in Sweden or go anywhere for you. Help me, Lord, to serve you and to never insist on always understanding everything you do. Teach me to obey without questioning and let me know the mystery of your Word."* Then, slowly, I fell asleep, right there on my knees..

From that day forward, I stopped fighting God. I knew I was where He wanted me to be and my life was in His hands. Being in Sweden was different and lonely at times, but, through it all, His hand was upon me. I was experiencing miracles each day of my life. Trials were not excluded in the walk of faith, though, but the miracles and blessings were greater than any problems I faced. Many souls were saved at the meetings I held, and God manifested His love in powerful ways. All this helped me endure any difficulty I faced. I continued living at Sveavagen 130 and went around preaching all over Scandinavia. Sister Mailis at the Bible School let me use the apartment because it became like a mission center. The one-month deal for the apartment changed. God was at work even when I wanted to do my own thing. I stopped struggling to go home and started living in His will.

After I received the message from the stranger that night, I asked God if He would allow me to go for a visit. He then allowed me to go to Tanzania after I made a vow to return to Sweden. I went home in 1978 and 1979 and held crusades and revival meetings in different churches. After the mission trips, I returned to Stockholm and continued working at the embassy.

As God took over my plans, my will, and my desires, life changed for me. I met many good Christian friends and families from different areas. The City Church in Stockholm became my home church with a big family. Pastor Stanley Sjorberg stood behind me in every project I did to win others for Christ. I started Friday night prayer meetings and late-night street walks with witnessing. Pastor allowed us to conduct the English services in the church facilities for the people who could not understand Swedish. Most of these people were saved in my house and on the streets. At first, the services were being held in my house, which the Lord had supernaturally provided.

When we outgrew it, we had to use the church. God was faithful. Remember this:

"Whoever sows sparingly will also reap sparingly, and whoever sows generously will also reap generously. Each man should give what he has decided in his heart to give, not reluctantly or under compulsion, for God loves a cheerful giver. And God is able to make all grace abound to you, so that in all things at all times, having all that you need, you will abound in every good work." (2 Corinthians 9:6-8)

Indeed, God is able to use any Christian to spread the Good News. He uses ordinary people who are willing to live by faith and obey Him. When you speak His Word, you have a promise that His Word "will not return to Him empty but will accomplish what He desires and achieve the purpose..." (Isaiah 55:11).

God has been very good to me, and I praise Him for calling me by name at a very early age. God knows His plan and purpose for each of His children. He stands ready to fulfill those plans. Have you considered what God's will is for your life? I know He has a specific plan for you. If God can reveal some of His desires for my life, He can do much more for you. If you are not sure, remember, all of us are required to love God and obey Him. This can be accomplished if we surrender our lives to Jesus Christ.

Chapter **10**

My Second Visit to Tanzania, 1979

As I obeyed God by not running away from the mission field, I continued to evangelize as much as I could. At the same time, I kept the needs of my people before Him. The wages I received by helping at the embassy was kept to buy things for the needy in Tanzania. God made provisions for me to return to help my people every year. I would buy clothes, music tapes, books, etc. Some friends would contribute financially for my trips to Tanzania. Often times, it was difficult to travel from one part of the region to another without transportation or money. Nevertheless, the gifts of those who gave toward spreading the Gospel helped. My family at home also gave their all to see me accomplish God's vision and mission.

I continued to hold revival meetings and crusades. The trip I took from November 4, 1979, to January 14, 1980, was filled with meetings. I traveled to many parts of Tanzania holding crusades and conducting seminars. One night, a lady came to receive Christ. She requested prayer because she was sick. Her stomach was swollen. Her husband was not a Christian and used to abuse her. As she finished talking, I held her stomach and prayed. Then I told her, "You are healed. Go home; your husband will not beat you. Tell him about the meeting and that you are a new person." God was faithful to confirm His Word with miracles.

The following day, the lady came back healed and brought her husband. He also got saved. I am always amazed and thrilled at how God does His work. It is a great feeling to depend upon Him.

Souls were being saved every time I ministered under the power of the Holy Spirit. Those who were tormented by all kinds of sicknesses were healed; those oppressed by demonic powers were set free.

We moved to another area for open-air crusades. God's power was so real! I remember a particular lady who came to the meeting at Kimara. As I was making the altar call, God showed her to me and revealed that she needed special prayer. She came forward and received Jesus Christ as her personal Lord and Savior. After prayers, I asked, "What more do you want to receive from God?" When she started to explain what she needed, I was almost sorry I asked!

"Preacher," she said, "I am afraid my husband will kill me tonight." I asked her why she would say that, and she explained in more detail. "My husband drinks so heavily and beats me every day. We are Muslims, and I was not supposed to be here, but something made me come. If he hears, he will kill me. Please go with me and talk to my husband." She spoke with tears rolling down her cheeks.

As I listened to her pain and agony, my heart went out to her. She did not look well. She was very thin and weak. At that moment, though, I did not have faith for her nor time to minister one-on-one with her. It was like my mind was too tired to pay closer attention. But as she showed me the swollen arm from the previous night's beating, I could feel the pain in her arm. My heart was inflamed with anger at the devil and horror at the man who did it. My faith was charged, and I stretched my hands and started praying for her and the swollen arm. I commanded God's healing power to flow and heal her right there. My anger toward the devil seemed to generate faith that God was going to do a miracle.

In His Great Commission in Mark 16:18, Jesus said, "... They will place their hands on sick people, and they will get well." I had confidence that God would honor His Word. Then I prayed for her husband to be saved.

After I finished praying for her and her husband, I said to her, "Go home, your husband will not beat you tonight or any other night—ever! He also will not drink alcohol again. The Jesus Christ you have accepted today will work in your husband's life, just go home praising God for the miracles."

These words flowed through my mouth as if it were someone else speaking. I knew then, and I know now, those words of faith were not my own but the Holy Spirit revealing and speaking them through me. He knew where her husband was, and I am sure He started convicting him before she arrived home.

There are times when I get mad with the deception of the enemy. As children of God, we need to get mad with the devil and block him from interfering with our lives.

"In your anger do not sin: Do not let the sun go down while you are still angry, and do not give the devil a foothold." (Ephesians 4: 26-27)

In my experience, many people whom I have counseled or ministered to have had problems that were the result of not knowing the power that God had given to them. They believed the devil's lies instead of the Word of God. The devil is a liar; do not give him any room in your heart or mind. Satan lost the battle two thousand years ago when Jesus rose from the dead. We have to remind him of that. Know who you are in God, for "... you are from God and have overcome them, because the one who is in you is greater than the one who is in the world" (1 John 4:4).

Two days later, I finished the meeting at the Kimara Assemblies of God and went to another area for another crusade. One day, just before I went on to the platform at Ilala Girls School grounds, a charming lady rushed up and said, "Preacher, I want you to meet my husband. He wants to get what you gave me." I could not recall what I had given her. Then she went on to say, "When I left the Kimara meeting after you prayed, the swelling on my arm disappeared that very day."

I did not realize who she was until she mentioned the Kimara crusade. She had changed. She now looked strong and healthy. I smiled and waited for her to continue.

"My husband says he cannot drink anymore," she said. "He has tried, but every time he drinks he throws up. When he gets angry and frustrated, he comes to beat me, but something pulls him away. Since that day when you prayed, he cannot strike me. He thinks I have gone to a medicine man, but I told him about you and your Jesus."

She was very excited explaining the changes that had taken place in her life and in her husband's life. It was a joy to see how God demonstrated His love to them. Unfortunately, I could not stay and listen long. I had to cut her testimony short because the meeting had already started. I told her we would talk more after the meeting.

With encouragement in my spirit, I preached and souls received Christ and others testified of being healed. Indeed, the lady's husband also gave his life to Christ that day. Although they were Muslims all their lives, they realized they needed Christ because He is the ONLY way and the truth and the life (John 14:6). They were willing to receive the prayer of faith that was offered on their behalf. Their faith in Christ activated miracles to happen in their lives. God is the one who sees your heart and He can do "exceeding abundantly above all that we ask or think, according to the power that worketh in us" (Ephesians 3:20). The power lies in you to release God's miracle that you need.

Once again, God taught me that it is not for me to understand all that the Spirit is directing me to say or to do, but rather to obey and act upon that "Rhema" word— God's specific word or instruction to me. What I told that particular lady concerning her alcoholic husband did not make sense to me. I did not tell this to any other lady who had a similar situation. It was a Rhema word to me for her. If a man had been drinking for years, how could I expect him to quit over night? Psychologists talk about the different stages one has to go through before one stops drinking. That is the worldly way. But our God is above natural reality. What does not make sense to us makes sense to Him, if it is in accordance with His word.

According to some popular theory of counseling, when the lady told me her problems, I should have slowly allowed her to have inner healing sessions for the abuses she endured through the years. I should have informed her it would be a while before healing could be expected and that she would need counseling for a period of time. That is the logical and human way.

But praise God He is not man. He is God. He can do an instant healing in any area of one's life, or He can heal by several methods, according to Scripture. Incidentally, I do understand that if God has not directed you otherwise, human methods and logic have to be applied; that is the reason God has given us intellect. The important factor we must realize is that God can do what He wills. No mortal being can dictate to Him or can understand all of His ways. Scripture says,

"Where is the wise man? Where is the scholar? Where is the philosopher of this age? Has not God made foolish the wisdom of the world? For the foolishness of God is wiser than man's wisdom, and the weakness of God is stronger than man's strength." (1 Corinthians 1:20, 25)

Through experience, I have learned not to label how God is going to do something but only to trust and obey. God will do what He has promised in His Word. That Muslim lady came by faith. She believed and received total healing. Above that, her husband's life changed, and he was different from that very day. Two weeks later, he confessed Jesus as his personal Lord and Savior and had no side effects or withdrawal from alcohol. He was changed and became a new person. This confirmed what 2 Corinthians 5:17 says, "Therefore, if any man be in Christ, he is a new creature, old things are passed away. Behold, all things are become new." Believe the supernatural will happen in your life. It does not matter whether it is physical, financial, or whatever! God will do it.

When we keep faith in God's Word, there should be no room for the obstacles of doubt and fear, yet that is often the case. You have seen in my story how often I had doubts and fear. As human beings, we tend to doubt what God speaks to us through His Word. When you do that, do not let the devil accuse you that you are good for nothing! Instead, let your doubt and fear prompt you to seek God. During that period of time in 1979, there were so many miracles that I thought I would never doubt God again. I sincerely believed that whatever God told me, I would obey without question. That was not the case. Before the cock could crow twice, so to speak, I started doubting and asking, "Is it You, Lord, saying I should go?"

Chapter 11

Trip to Zambia

During the Kimara meeting, some people from Zambia came to me and said, "God has directed us to ask you to come to Zambia to preach." I told them it was impossible. I had so many other meetings in Tanzania. They insisted that God had spoken to them that I should go. Politely, I looked at them and said, "My schedule is too tight. I cannot accommodate any meeting outside Tanzania." I went further and jokingly said, "Brothers, I understand your desire to have me in your country, but I am sure God forgot that Zambia was too far away, and I cannot afford to come there at this time."

They did not pay attention to what I was telling them and insisted that I should go. I did not pay any further attention to their request either. Realistically, I knew it was impossible at that particular time.

I continued with different meetings and forgot about Zambia. After a few weeks, I heard that still, small voice, saying, "Daughter, go to Zambia." Oh, how I hated to hear that! It was as if I had never heard Him send me anywhere before. Somehow in my natural mind, I hated when God did that to me. Can you relate to what I am saying—when it seems God gives orders without warning you?

I had never been to Zambia before, and I did not want the Swedish trip experience to be revived again. Moreover, when those brothers were talking with me, I did not bother to take their names or addresses. It's not unusual for people to ask an evangelist to speak in his or her area. I thought it was one of those requests, so I did not pay much attention to it.

When God spoke again, I started thinking. I knew two things about these three brothers: They came and sang at the meetings, they had beautiful voices, and the singing that they did during the crusade was inspiring. The other thing that I knew was the place they came from. They were brothers from Kitwe in Zambia. I did not know anything else. Knowing about their voices and their town did not help me plan for a trip. The more I thought about it, the more I dismissed the idea. I was not sure He was sending me. These thoughts kept coming to me—*How can I just go? Why did God not impress on me to take their address?*

I battled with logic and the reality of the situation. It did not make sense. However, I took the first step to obey

God by asking people if anyone had the address of the Zambian brothers. But no one did. Then I concluded that it must not have been God telling me to go to Zambia; otherwise, He would have provided a proper contact for me. Looking for a contact was sensible. I was ready to go if I could find someone to contact so they could start preparing for the meetings. It was logical and sensible to inform someone that I was coming. In this situation, I did not even have the names of the singing brothers, nor their addresses, and I concluded I was not to go.

I continued with my schedule. Two days passed, and I started booking the train for Mwanza (northwest of Tanzania) to go for crusades that were on the schedule. In my spirit, there was a strong sense of urgency, but I could not figure it out. Then I heard God say, "Nicku, you are not going northwest, but you are going south to Zambia." When I heard that, it was vivid and I could doubt and question no more! It was then that I had to obey and say, "Yes, Lord," to His will and call.

There are times when I know without any possible doubt that God is speaking. Then I leave everything and avail myself of His direction. This was one of those instances that I had no doubt. There are other times when I am not sure, and I have to wait or try to dismiss the idea. If it continues, then I try to pray and meditate until I hear again. And there are times when I know it is Him, but I try to persuade Him not to say what He is saying or not to send me where I do not know anyone. I become spiritual by praying and fasting in order to persuade Him to change His mind.

In most cases, it is because I want to follow my ways rather than His. Our spiritual rituals do not impress God. He sees our hearts and the motives behind our prayers, fasting, giving alms. Whatever we do, God knows.

"Serve Him with wholehearted devotion and with a willing mind, for the Lord searches every heart and understands every motive behind the thoughts..." (1 Chronicles 28:91)

Although I had no specific direction on how to reach the brothers in Kitwe, Zambia, I had to start moving. By faith, I knew God wanted me to step out and expect Him to lead me a day at a time. I changed the train reservation and headed south to Zambia instead of northwest to Mwanza. Indeed,

"A man's steps are directed by the Lord. How then can anyone understand his own way?" (Proverbs 20:24)

What a paradox! Although God has led me to several places without my having any contacts, I still question and fight with the call when it comes. It is hard to obey beyond the obvious, yet that is what we have to do.

"For my thoughts are not your thoughts, neither are your ways my ways." declares the Lord. 'As the heavens are higher than the earth, so are my ways higher than your ways and my thoughts than your thoughts." (Isaiah 55:8-9)

I am learning each day to walk by faith and not by sight. The following day when people came to see me off they could not understand why I was on a different train. There was no need for explanation. I knew they would not understand. I left them wondering.

The two days in the train to Tunduma, a town that borders Tanzania and Zambia, were glorious. I had time to pray and witness. Three people were saved, many more heard the Good News, and one received the baptism of the Holy Spirit in my cabin. When we arrived at the border, the train to Kapili Mposhi had already left. The schedule had changed, and we could not ride it because there was war in Rhodesia (now Zimbabwe), and Zambia was affected. An enemy bombed a portion of the trail, and the train could not reach Kapili Mposhi. All passengers had to continue their journey in buses the following day.

When our train from Dar es Salaam had to stay in Tunduma, we were told we had to spend a night there then take buses early in the morning based on our destinations. Many people were left to sleep at the station. I went to spend the night with my brother on the Tanzanian side of the border. It was a blessing because I had not seen him for a long time. We shared what I had done in Sweden and about our family in Dar es Salaam. When he asked about the trip to Kitwe, I hesitated to hint about God's leading. But somehow I found myself telling him everything. To my surprise, he was not shocked. The only thing he told me was, "If God said so, He will prepare someone for you. Be careful."

The following morning, as my brother and his wife escorted me across the border to catch the bus, we found out the bus left two hours earlier. It was frustrating because we were told the bus from Tunduma on the Zambian side was leaving at 8:30 to go to Kitwe, but when we arrived at 8:15, the bus had already left. It was annoying because I had to sit at the bus stop and just wait without having an idea when the next bus would leave. This is when my brother changed his mind. He decided it might not be such a good idea after all. He kept trying to convince me that I should not go. He could not understand my faith. If it was God, then the obstacles should not be there, he thought.

My brother wanted to know how could He be sending me during a time of war. He was getting angry because I would not listen to his advice. I kept on praying and waiting. At times I wished he would leave.

The fear I had the previous night, of not wanting to tell him the whole truth, became a reality. He did not want his little sister to be naïve. He wanted to convince me that God was not in this. I respected his concern, but I could not obey him because God had spoken to me before my brother was even in the picture. I had to trust God in spite of the circumstances that we were facing.

We were at the bus station without a clue as to when we would leave. My brother and his wife had to leave me there. Before he left, he said, "We will be happy if you change your mind. You can come back home." They left without saying good-bye.

I kept on checking to see when the next bus was coming. My mission had to be accomplished; there was no thought of going back home. Later, I discovered why they did not give people the exact time of the departures. Because of the war, bus schedules were not made public; this helped to avoid sabotage and any danger to the passengers. Security and transport officials left people waiting for hours while they checked to make sure that all was safe. Our time came finally, and we boarded the bus.

As we entered Zambia, freedom fighters were everywhere. The army also had roadblocks everywhere. The situation was very tense because several bombings were going on in different parts of the country. The bus had to use several detours and passengers were checked. We passed through thick forest without any food. In some areas, people would look for food, but they could only find sugar cane. Sometimes in the rain we had to go on foot for miles while the driver drove an empty bus. This was to protect the passengers and avoid enemies who might want to attack the bus. It was the hardest mission trip I had ever encountered.

When thoughts of doubt and fear came, the Spirit would remind me of God's call and bring His word to remembrance.

"I am with you and will watch over you wherever
you go, and I will bring you back to this land;
I will not leave you until I have done what I
have promised you." (Genesis 28:151)

Through the hardship, God continued to reveal that His plans were never a mistake. On that bus, I shared Christ. People wanted to know who I was and about my mission to Zambia. Souls got saved, and they received hope for the future in spite of the uncertainty. Soldiers at roadblocks who were checking the bus and passengers were witnessed to as they asked me why I was in Zambia. When they checked my passport, it was written, "Evangelist," and some wanted to know what it meant and what I did. Opportunity upon opportunity was at my disposal to tell them about Christ.

At one checkpoint, however, the soldiers were very skeptical. They could not believe that a female evangelist would go to preach in the midst of war. One commented that I was on a different mission with a religious cover up. They had caught several people who said they were priests but were really mercenaries. But my nationality helped them know I would not be on the enemy's side. They stopped interrogating me.

At that time, the driver rearranged the passengers in my favor. He did not want anyone to bother me. He even sent all those who smoked to sit at the back of the bus. People obeyed the driver willingly and respected my beliefs. He called me to sit near him. I was given a seat to myself instead of sharing with two other people. When we reached my checkpoint, he spoke on my behalf in their language.

It was as if God appointed the bus crew as my bodyguards. They treated me with respect and told others to do likewise. When we got to checkpoints, no one opened my bags. When passengers were ordered to go out, I was told to remain inside the bus. Soldiers followed me in the bus to look at my passport. After inspecting it, they would say, "Pray for us," as they gave it back to me. It was a terrible time for everyone, but on that journey, ten passengers got saved. All glory and honor I give to God!

"Since then, we know what it is to fear the Lord, we try to persuade men. What we are is plain to God ... God was reconciling the world to himself in Christ ... And He has committed to us the message of reconciliation. We are therefore Christ's ambassadors...." (2 Corinthians 5:11, 19-20)

When I arrived in Kitwe, six days had passed since I had left Tanzania by train. I did not know what to do next. I was tired and dirty but not hungry. Since I had been fasting, it was fine for me to travel without food.

I disembarked and stood looking around. In my spirit, I was communicating with God. It was not easy to get off the bus knowing I had no contact. Still, I knew God was in control. He proved that through my journey to Kitwe. Remembering the people who got saved in the bus and the soldiers who were asking for prayers reminded me to expect another miracle.

As I looked around while praying, one person came to ask me where I was going. He recognized my sunglasses and wanted to know if I was the same person in the train from Dar es Salaam who had been preaching. When I told him I was, he wondered why I was arriving four days later. He traveled in the same train and made the connection to Kitwe the same day. I told him I missed the bus at the border.

"I am not sure where I am going," I continued. "My first mission is to contact some brothers who had invited me to conduct some meetings in Kitwe."

"That is no problem," he replied. "I will take you there." But when he asked for their names or addresses and realized I did know them, he was astonished. "Now that is a problem! You are in Kitwe alright, but you need to start from somewhere."

Unfortunately, I did not know where to start or what to say to him. Shocked, he turned to me and said, "I would not know either."

He kept silent for a moment and then he remembered what made him approach me.

"As I was driving by and saw you, I felt I needed to come to talk with you. As I approached you, I recognized that I had seen you in the train." He put his hand on his chin and continued, "Now I know why I had to come. You need help, and I will try to help you."

He took my luggage, and we went to his car. I praised God for the faithfulness of this gentleman and thanked him for being willing to take me. He was indeed a Good Samaritan.

As we drove and talked, he decided to take me to a family that I could stay with while I looked for my contacts. He went in and talked with them. The lady came out; she was kind and took me in. When I shared God's mission and why I was there, she had the same look as everyone else: *How could you leave your country to come here without having names of people to meet you?* She might have thought something different; nevertheless, her look was one of surprised concern. Then she asked if I knew the name of the church where they might worship. I told her I did not. She replied, "Well, we will see. Having the names would have been helpful." Indeed, she was right.

In this modern world, you have to make plans before you do anything. However, I was there without a clue about anything except obedience to God's command: "Go!" This is what the early Christians did. They went to spread the Gospel without depending on their ability or "know-how." Those men and women depended on God's instructions and they availed themselves to go wherever

God sent them. Today, the Church is marching on because of the people before who walked in faith. God is looking for your availability to win the lost at all costs. He will use you for His glory if you will only trust Him and obey.

Although I had no helpful information for anyone, I knew God was in control. I was content because of the people who accepted Christ in the train and in the bus and how He used the man who recognized my sunglasses. These were all signs of encouragement to me. I kept on praying and praising God saying, *"Lord, if my mission trip was for those souls and for me to learn more of your ways as in Psalm 23, I thank you, and I am ready to go back home."* I felt my mission was complete.

But after being with the family for three days, God's supernatural power was manifested once again. One day, my host took me to a house prayer meeting. When we entered, I was overwhelmed to see the Christian brothers who attended the crusade in Tanzania. They stood to hug me and could not believe I was there. No one told them I was around because no one knew who I was. Plus, I told them I could not make it to Zambia because my schedule was tight! Needless to say, we rejoiced together.

While at the prayer meeting, I learned the nine-year-old daughter of one of the attendees was in the hospital. The mother shared with me that the prayer meeting was for her daughter. The child had been suffering from bone cancer since she was five years old. The doctors had been treating her for a long period of time without success.

That week, the doctors presented the mother with two options: Either avoid amputation and her child would die from cancer, or amputate the leg up to the knee before the cancer spread further and affected other parts of her body.

When I heard the story and saw the mother's pain and anguish for her child, I was filled with compassion. One of the brothers testified about the healings he saw when he attended the crusade in Dar es Salaam. Our faith was uplifted. After we finished the prayers, I asked her if I could go to the hospital and pray for her daughter. She was very happy, and we left accompanied by two other brothers.

As we entered the hospital room, I had the strangest feeling. Suddenly I realized it was not because I was in a foreign country with strangers, but because the Holy Spirit was assuring me that there would be no operation on the girl. I was afraid to tell them what the Spirit of God was communicating to me: "There would be no operation nor amputation. God has already healed her."

Logic told me it was not proper to say what God was revealing to me. How could I appear there from another country and tell the mother not to worry because her daughter was healed? What if she was not healed? Fear overcame me, and I tried to reason with myself in order to avoid speaking what God was saying. *What would people say if it did not happen? How can I just come to these people and say that the child is healed? What about those who have prayed for her since she was five years old? Why did God not heal her then? Who am I to speak to a mother who has prayed for many years and not seen anything happen?* Many more thoughts kept flashing through my mind. As I continued to battle over the right decision, it seemed logical not to say a word.

The devil always brings questions and doubts to prevent us from trusting what God tells us through His word. The devil knows that if we disobey God, we will not receive what God has in store for us. The devil plants doubt in our minds and then we start disobeying God's Word. He did that in the garden when he told Eve, "Did God really say, 'You must not eat from the tree in the gardens?'" (Genesis 3:1). He continued to plant doubt until Eve yielded to temptation.

I know this to be true. Do you recall how the devil misquoted God's Word the time he tempted Jesus in the desert? He said, "If you are the Son of God …" (Luke 4:3ff). Sometimes the devil works by causing you to fear walking by faith. He wants you to doubt what the word of God says. He likes to twist God's Word so you will doubt God. I have fallen in that trap many times. I do not accept things that do not make sense immediately—like making a mission trip without any contact.

Nevertheless, I praise God because He never gives up on us when we question sincerely. He has been patient with me. He knows we are children who are weak and sometimes stumble in our faith. He is always near, listening to hear us say, "Lord, we are weak. Take over when we do not understand; lead us. We surrender to you."

As we walked inside the hospital ward to see the sick child, I felt the Holy Spirit move inside me strongly, and I found myself saying what I thought could not be spoken. I looked at the group and said, "Mother, and you brothers who are here, this girl is healed in Jesus's name. Now we will just thank God for the miracle. The cancer is gone already." With confidence, I went onto say, "God showed it to me as we came into the room." The lady had such faith that she said only, "Thank you, Lord, I receive it for my child."

One man looked at me surprised, but I felt I said what God wanted me to say. As we entered the room, I went to the girl, put my hands on her leg and chest. I started to thank God for the miracle. We all praised God and left the hospital.

The next day, they arranged for a meeting in one of the schools. God confirmed His word with souls accepting Christ, and through healings of common sicknesses such as colds and headaches. Above all, others received faith to trust what God says. With my mission complete, I left for Tanzania the following day.

As I rode the bus and then the train to Tanzania, my mind was on the hospital. The girl's condition could not escape my thoughts. I arrived home with feelings of death and dissatisfaction. I was not sure why I felt the heaviness, but it was there.

When I was going to Zambia, I knew God sent me for a purpose. I felt I had accomplished the mission. *Then why the heaviness?* I wondered. I often prayed and longed to hear something about the little girl, but no report came from Kitwe. I felt like a failure, and I was ashamed.

The devil discovered a weakness in my confidence and kept telling me that my prayer in the hospital was never answered and that I brought shame to my God. The accusations continued: *People will say that an evangelist from Tanzania pretended that God said the cancer was gone when, in fact, it was not!* Many embarrassing thoughts flashed in my mind, and I entertained them. I should have practiced 1 Peter 5:9, which says, "Resist him, stand firm in the faith."

The devil is the accuser; he was using my own mind to make me doubt God's promise. Many times when the devil comes to tempt us in words or deeds, we allow him. I allowed him to do so that time. Instead of binding him and reminding him of God's Word, I worried and became concerned about the healing, wondering whether it did happen. I should have remembered what I learned through experience—that it is not the evangelist or the preacher that heals but God. My duty was to obey God's instructions no matter how impossible it seemed.

If there is a need for healing, we are called to pray for the sick and believe, for nothing is impossible with God. In this case at the hospital, I was to pronounce the healing and expect the manifestation of it. The devil planted fear in me, and I welcomed it. The feeling of death the devil planted in my spirit continued for a long time. I could not understand why it was there.

The time came for me to leave Tanzania to continue my mission in Sweden without ever hoping to hear from anyone in Kitwe about the child. I thought the worst had happened and no one would ever trust me as called of God. However, in early February, after I had returned to Sweden, I received a letter from the mother of the girl. When I saw it, I opened it quickly and read it. It was a joy to hear that the child was healed and discharged from the hospital three days after I had left. "My child's healing was a miracle and a testimony to all," she said.

I was so happy to receive that letter and the news it contained. I praised God because He never fails. I had to confess and repent for having doubted. At the same time, I blamed myself for listening to the devil and wasting time by having vain imaginations of how people would feel if what I told them did not come to pass.

The devil wants us to have quick answers. That is not how God works. His promises are all "Yes" and "Amen" if we walk in the Spirit of God all the time. It is not our ability that brings about God's will but our obedience to His instructions. Waiting in limbo can be difficult, but when God says, "Wait," one has to wait for His timing. He knows what is best for you. The assignment He gave me and the delayed information helped me realize that.

Although God told me He had healed the child before I saw her, the circumstances brought doubt.

I wrote the mother with excitement, promising to visit again when God was through with me in Sweden. I believe God's healing power can flow through any child of His. We are only vessels, which He is ready to use as long as we are willing to be available and obedient. Above all, God uses us at His own timing. We have to rely upon His power daily.

Consider the case of Peter. At one moment, he had so much faith and was available for God to use him to reveal who Jesus was, "You are the Christ, the Son of the Living God" (Matthew 16:16). Just a few hours later, it was the same Peter who was used by the devil. Jesus had to say to him, "Get behind me, Satan!" (Matthew 16:23).

As human beings, we have to surrender to God's way all the time. We should never dwell on how God used us yesterday but on how He uses us today. Yesterday's "manna" cannot be used today (Read Exodus 16:11-20). In other words, if God uses you, do not be content with just those accomplishments; seek Him daily for a fresh move of His Spirit so that you can enjoy new accomplishments with Him.

Jesus told Peter that God revealed to him the understanding of who He was (Matthew 16:16-17). Indeed, God used Peter but the devil used him, too. We need to walk in the Spirit of God all the time. It is not our ability that brings victory, but our availability and total surrender to God's will for our lives.

Chapter 12

Tragedy In My Family

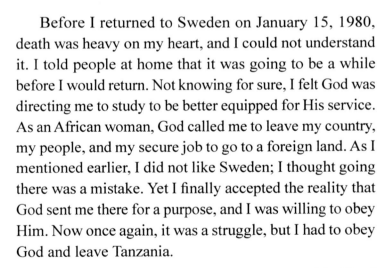

Before I returned to Sweden on January 15, 1980, death was heavy on my heart, and I could not understand it. I told people at home that it was going to be a while before I would return. Not knowing for sure, I felt God was directing me to study to be better equipped for His service. As an African woman, God called me to leave my country, my people, and my secure job to go to a foreign land. As I mentioned earlier, I did not like Sweden; I thought going there was a mistake. Yet I finally accepted the reality that God sent me there for a purpose, and I was willing to obey Him. Now once again, it was a struggle, but I had to obey God and leave Tanzania.

In those early days back in Sweden, I felt like I was saying goodbye to my homeland for good. There were times when I wondered why God would place me in a country where everything was cold. Life in the churches was cold in comparison with my African home churches. Even in the homes, people did not talk with each other like I was accustomed to. Sweden was a lonely place for an African like me.

At that point in my Christian pilgrimage, I did not understand why God took me there. If my love for Jesus was dependent upon people, especially while in the mission field, I am sure I could have stopped going to churches. Above all, I could have stopped being a living witness for Christ everywhere I went. But I was a Christian who was not ashamed of the Gospel of Jesus Christ (Romans 1:16). The fact that God brought me there gave me determination to witness for Him.

When you follow God's path, every place He sends you can be accommodating. The vision I saw at the age of six kept me going many times. I was able to endure all hardships and loneliness. I knew the promise that says, "Lo! I am with you always, even unto the end of the world" (Matthew 28:20). I tasted and found that the Lord is good, and He is faithful. True, I had unpleasant experiences when I first arrived in Sweden, but people are people and they will fail us; yet Jesus is Lord, and *He never fails*!

There was no doubt that everything in Sweden was different from my culture. Even evidence and reality indicated I was crazy to be there! But I knew I was there on a mission, no matter how much I had to adjust to accomplish His purpose. Often, I tried to express the African charm and hospitality. I did it because I wanted to express God's love to people. Everywhere I went, any person I talked with, I told them about His grace and love. God used me to touch lives in different ways. Many accepted Christ and were delivered from the chains of the enemy.

Although the Swedish people are very kind and friendly, it takes a long time for a foreigner to discover their friendliness. At least that was my experience. Most of the time, I was in Christian meetings and churches, but I did not have much fellowship outside the church. Most people were shy. Most people were not interested in having social fellowship after services. Each went his or her way as soon as the service was over. Even so, I met a few who became friends with me.

After a year and a half, however, I discovered I had more friends than I thought. I praise God for every family and friend I have in Sweden. The City Church Assembly became my real home away from home. I began bringing the English-speaking people there and introduced them to the pastor. Pastor Stanley was always willing to meet and minister to all.

It was encouraging to have a pastor who was willing to implement some of the things I would suggest. For example, on Friday nights we started prayer and street witnessing in downtown Stockholm. We would go to the underground train stations and other places where drug addicts, prostitutes, alcoholics, and those who roamed the streets aimlessly could be found. These people were our target. While we did that, another group continued to have prayers in the church. God was with us as we went for midnight evangelism. Each night, we would lead someone to Christ. Those who accepted Christ were encouraged to follow us to the church and special prayers were offered for them. Most of them refused to follow us, but others came and received prayer and God's special love.

Those English-speaking people we met in the streets or other places were encouraged to attend the English Sunday service at 1 p.m. It was a blessing to see many touched by God's power. A time came after my most recent trip to Tanzania that I finally felt that I belonged in Sweden. I wanted to learn the Swedish language, so I could witness to every one in the streets, not just to English-speaking people. As I continued to evangelize, it became obvious why God brought me there. Many doors were opening for ministry, and I had no immediate intention to return to Tanzania. The harvest was plentiful but the workers were few. God had placed me in that vineyard. I was determined to serve Him at all cost.

One particular Friday night, we went to witness on the streets at 10 p.m. I stood outside a movie theater with two other people. Another group stood outside the restaurant. Almost every person with whom we talked was very receptive to the Gospel. One man knelt outside the theater with tears running down his face. He was contemplating committing suicide that night, but God saved him from death. Six were saved that night. We were excited and did not pay much attention to the time. After a while, we looked at our watches and discovered it was 3 a.m. Then we decided to go and get some sleep. Two girls came to stay with me, while Pastor Stanley and another person went back to the church and then home. Our hearts were rejoicing, fulfilled spiritually because of the souls that were saved.

That next morning, I was awakened at around 8 a.m. by a telephone call. When I took the receiver, it was my sister Enjo calling from Tanzania. "Nicku," she said, "we tried to call you several times yesterday, but you were not in." She sighed and continued, "Please come home immediately. Mother is sick." She went on to tell me that my ticket with Tanzania Airways was waiting for me in London.

What I needed to do was purchase a ticket from Stockholm to London, connect the flight, and then I would be in Africa on Wednesday. I knew something was not right. In my family, we never telephone someone far away to tell about an illness. As I tried to question her, she put down the receiver. I could tell she was crying. She did not want me to know that my mother had gone to be with the Lord. At the same time, I could not imagine it would be *Mom*. Although I knew my sister had called to give me "bad news," I tried to focus on someone else.

Since she hung up without finishing her instructions, I tried to call back, but I could not find anyone at home. Then I called a friend's home in Dar es Salaam. A child about ten years old answered.

"Let me speak to your Mom or Dad," I asked.

"They are not in," he replied.

"Where have they gone?" I asked.

"They have gone to aunty. Her mother has died."

"Which aunty?" I asked quickly.

"Mama Ulli," he answered.

I cannot explain how I felt. Mama Ulli was the sister who had called me. The boy confirmed that my mother had died. I was devastated. The ground seemed to open underneath my feet, and the whole world seemed to collapse.

I screamed, I shouted, I paced the floor, shouting, "Oh no! Why?" The girls who spent the night with me could not believe I was the same person who was always so full of faith and courage, a person who testified about how God used her in many ways.

I was their mentor, and they were proud to call me their friend. They saw me preach under God's anointing. Even the previous eight hours when we were on the street witnessing, they saw how God used me to reach the people with the message of hope and love through Christ. They saw how we ushered six souls into God's Kingdom! Yet, here I was, screaming without faith or hope. They did not know what to think or what to say; they just watched!

After a while, I calmed down and called an embassy official to inform him about my mother's death, and I asked them if they could possibly purchase an airline ticket for me. "Not now," the official said. It was Saturday. They could do nothing until Monday. Then he went onto say, "Let us wait until Monday. We can discuss the matter in the office."

But waiting was impossible for me. I walked up and down my Sveavagen apartment crying. *How can I wait while my mother is dead?* I screamed the more and threw myself on the bed. Then I remembered there was a KLM flight that left Stockholm Saturday at noon for Tanzania. I lifted myself up and went to the living room. I told my visitors that I was going home that morning. They could stay and lock the place up when they were ready to leave.

The atmosphere was very tense as they watched me. They were so scared because they had never experienced anything like that before. The screaming and questioning God about why my mother died did not portray the faith I professed. Normally, when Christians die, people have the faith to say, "It is God's will, and we will see them again. The Bible promises that the departed loved ones have gone to a better place." For those who are left behind, it should be a time of rejoicing. A celebration for a "home-going victory."

For me, there was no faith at that time, and I did not want to rejoice. I did not thank God either; instead, I was angry with Him. As I cried, I could not stop asking him why, but no answer came.

As I was ready to walk out the door, I told the girls I was going to the airport. I asked them to inform the pastor and other friends that I left. I only had a handbag and my overnight bag. They looked at me and did not say a word. I am sure they thought I was joking. Without a ticket in my hand and no reservation, I left the apartment and headed for the airport.

When I arrived, someone at the entrance asked, "Where are you going, Nicku?" At first, I did not recognize her. I wondered who she was, but I went ahead and told her about the tragedy. She took me to the counter and bought a ticket for me without my requesting it. It was a miracle! God put her there for me at the right time. But at that moment, I did not think it was a miracle. I was too heartbroken to notice what God was doing in my situation.

When I reached the airport in Amsterdam, Holland, I went to the transit desk as usual. I gave them my ticket but could not find my passport. When the ground stewardess on the transfer desk asked for it, I replied, "My mother has died, and I do not have the passport." They said nothing as they gave me the ticket. I went to the gate and left for Tanzania. God was in control in spite of my anger or lack of faith.

At that time, I was not thinking anything was a miracle. I was too sad to spiritualize anything. Looking back, I realize it was divine intervention—how I left the apartment to head for the airport, the way I got the ticket, and traveling from Sweden to Tanzania without a passport was miraculous, too.

Unfortunately, I did not think in those terms. I was too angry and bitter with God. I had even sensed death during my mission trip to Zambia, but I could not understand why. *Why did not He tell me in advance that my mother was going to die?*

During the November 1979 to January 1980 crusades, I sensed something unusual. As I traveled in different places, I felt death. It was most pronounced on the trip to Zambia because of the war in the neighboring country. There was uncertainty of who might strike our bus; every passenger was anxious. I kept praying because I thought I might die without any of my family members' knowledge. Yet I had peace within me because my life rested in His hands.

"If we live, we live to the Lord, and if we die,
we die to the Lord. So whether we live or die,
we belong to the Lord." (Romans 14:8)

In that trip, we used rough roads and detours to avoid bombings on the main roads. We could have had an accident by trying to avoid the enemy. Indeed, it was a rough trip, and I felt death all over me. To me, that would have been the proper time for God to have told me, "Nicku, the death you sense is for your mother." It would have been painful, but I could have stayed in Tanzania and continued with meetings there until my mother passed away. I do not know how I would have reacted, but it would have been better for me to be home with her. There was no urgent need for me to return to Sweden except to serve God, and now He had let my mother die before I could see her for the last time. These thoughts continued and made me very depressed.

Although it was with anger and without faith or hope, I left Sweden three hours after I heard the news. God was directing every move. I took the KLM flight to Dar es Salaam. I had to travel over 900 miles by bus to reach my destination. Miraculously, I arrived in Mbeya, my hometown, on Monday, June 3, 1980.

Everything went so fast; it was miraculous. Our transportation was very poor. To make matters worse, the bus I took broke down. Under these circumstances, we would normally have to wait for hours, sometimes days. But on that day, I got a lift from several vehicles. I left other passengers behind. God was directing every step, but I knew it not. My devastation blinded my eyes, and I did not notice God's faithfulness. Instead of praising Him, I was angry with Him.

When I reached home and they saw me, no one could believe I was there so soon. Unfortunately, they had already buried my mother on Sunday afternoon. They were expecting me to arrive on Friday, but I came four days earlier. To hear she was already buried was devastating, and I did not know what to do. People who were gathered felt sad for me. "She could have paid her last respects if we had known she would arrive today," they said.

My family kept asking and wondering how I managed to come home so quickly. I did not want to start witnessing to them how miraculously God had brought me there. I did not even want to think or talk about God. I was still angry and bitter.

When people started singing, I would sing Christian songs and hymns with them. Traditionally, our funerals are dominated by singing rather than by crying. Sometimes tears flow when one meditates upon the words. However, my singing at that time was not communion with God nor was I meditating on the words. I was singing because everyone was singing. Above all, it was just a routine thing that people do at funerals.

For the first time in my life when I was faced with a tragedy, I did not want God and did not want to serve Him anymore. My mind kept questioning Him. *How can I serve a God who let me down? It was unfair for God not to be open with me. Why did He give me a hint of death during the mission trip if He was not going to be specific?*

During that crisis, I forgot what faith was all about. I forgot that as a child of God, and especially as a Minister of the Gospel, I should forsake all and trust Him in every situation. But I am the first one to admit that it is hard to remember the Word of God when a crisis hits. Nevertheless, God's love remains the same, and the Holy Spirit continues to intercede for us:

"The Spirit helps us in our weaknesses. We do not know what we ought to pray but the Spirit himself intercedes for us with groans that words cannot express." (Romans 8:26)

I praise God because I know He did not give up on me, and He will never give up on you. After mourning for three weeks with my family, I went back to Sweden. My intention was to get there, pack up my things, and return home to be with my father. Physically, spiritually, mentally, and emotionally, I was much weaker and more hopeless than when I had left Stockholm for the funeral. Sorrow and depression increased, leaving a perfectly open door for the enemy to oppress me.

I started contemplating suicide instead of going back home. *It would be impossible for me to live any other life apart from serving God, and since I do not want Him, the only way that seems logical is to die.* This thought kept running through my mind. Life without my mother seemed unbearable.

Revival meetings were going on in my Stockholm Church. I tried to go, but I became sadder. I could not stand seeing people praise a God who had been so unfair to me. To make matters worse, most people did not understand my dilemma. I obeyed Him, lived faithfully and seriously for Him, left all for His name's sake, yet I felt betrayed by Him. *Why could He not tell me that Mother was about to die? Is this what I get for serving Him?* Question upon question flooded my mind. I just could not bear the pain of that loss. My mother meant the world to so many; her sudden departure could not be understood.

I tried to go back to work at the embassy, but things became worse. My boss was not happy I stayed away for four weeks after Mother died. No one seemed to care. *Why should he be upset instead of sympathizing with me!* I was engrossed in my own pity-party.

Even if people did care, I did not notice because I was so busy feeling sorry for myself. I kept sinking deeper into depression, and I could not bear the pain. Once again, I started seriously planning suicide. The devil was very glad and quick to give me several suggestions.

First, he suggested I jump out from the bedroom window of my second floor apartment. When I looked, I knew if I jumped from there, I would only break my bones and not die. It was not far enough. I brushed the idea aside. The devil kept suggesting other methods to take my life. Indeed, "an idle mind is the devil's playground."

The following day, another idea came. *How about going to the seventh floor of your building? When you jump from there, you will be crushed and you would surely die.* "Oh, yes, that is a great idea," I responded, choosing to listen to the devil, my all-time enemy.

But I was low and frustrated, and his ideas sounded better than God's. In a crisis, I have seen the enemy bring thoughts and suggestions that might sound like quick solutions, but the end is destruction. Responding to an instant solution is natural, and many of us make this mistake over and over again. Entertaining the devil instead of God is tragic. Faith and patience are what God requires in situations like mine.

As you may know, the suicide rate in Sweden is very high. I did not want anyone to assume I died because of a boyfriend or something else; I did not want to be a statistic nor leave any room for speculation. I decided to leave a suicide note to explain why I was dying. The note read, *I am dying because my mother died and God has let me down*. I put the note on the dining room table for someone to find. I was planning to jump the next day, and I prepared everything and left the house clean. On my way to the seventh floor to commit suicide, God stepped in.

Chapter 13

"Daughter, Depart From Sweden"

No matter what you are going through, God can prepare a way out. He did it for me in Sweden, and He continues to do it. The Bible says,

"No temptation has seized you except what is common to man. And God is faithful, he will not let you be tempted beyond what you can bear. But when you are tempted, he will also provide a way out so that you can stand up under it." (1 Corinthians 10:13)

The hour to jump off the seventh floor had been well calculated. I started out the door when I remembered I did not close the bedroom window. I went back inside to lock the window. While I was pulling the window curtains, I heard the mailman drop something in my slot inside the apartment. When I went to see what it was, I saw a letter from Oral Roberts University in Tulsa, Oklahoma. I was incredulous. *Not today!*

I opened the letter. The first lines I read were, "Congratulations on being accepted at Oral Roberts University (ORU). Please report for school on August 18, 1980." The letter went on to say I would receive other documents if I paid the tuition fee of U.S. $5,450 per academic year or send half the amount for the first semester. They also needed a $100 non-refundable dorm deposit.

It was July 11, 1980, when the letter arrived. It was obvious the letter would have been missed if I had not gone back to lock the bedroom window. *Or could God have done something else?* I am sure He could.

I was shocked to receive that letter because I was not expecting any mail from the United States. Three years earlier, when I had not wanted to stay in Sweden, I applied to the school. The school admissions director wrote to say I was not accepted. Within my spirit, however, I sensed that God wanted me there, so I reapplied. Once again, they said I was not qualified to join the university.

After trying several times, I gave up the idea of being at ORU. I began to feel at peace in Sweden, knowing God brought me there for a purpose, especially after I had received the midnight call—"Nicku, do not run away from God." I knew God chose Sweden for me for His will.

"You did not choose me, but I chose you to go and bear fruit—fruit that will last. Then the Father will give you whatever you ask in my name." (John 15:16)

But when my mother died, I lost faith in God and in life. Yet, it was at that time that God's amazing loving care was demonstrated once again. In my helplessness, He stepped in.

"I will cleanse them from all the sin they have committed against me and will forgive all their sins of rebellion against me. Then this city will bring me renown joy, praise, and honor before all nations on earth that hear of all the good things I do for it; and they will be in awe and will tremble at the abundant prosperity and peace I provide for it." (Jeremiah 33:8-9)

God did not condemn me but rather loved me and brought a miracle. He taught me a lesson—that I do not have to be strong or spiritual when He shows His love; His love is *Agape*, the unconditional love. Above all, His grace and love toward us does not depend on how good we are, but on how sincere and serious we are to obey and follow Him. God sees what is inside of us.

"I the Lord search the heart and examine the mind, to reward the man according to his conduct." (Jeremiah 17:10)

I learned He is still the same God who cares for me whether I am weak or strong. Do not let the devil accuse you of not doing outward things. For over a month, I did not read my Bible or pray. Maybe the devil tried to convince me that I deserved to die because I had failed God! Praise God because He looks beyond the religious rituals. He sees your heart and the motive behind everything you do.

After reading the letter over and over again, I stood there gazing at the door, not believing I was accepted to ORU. I had one month to prepare and be there. For the first time since my mother died, I knelt down and said, "God, if you are there, if you are really there, you have to prove it to me now."

Because of the pain I was going through, it did not feel like God was there. I continued to say, "I want to leave Stockholm for the USA in three weeks with all the money I need to pay for the tuition." After saying that prayer, I got off my knees. Imagine, instead of going to the seventh floor to end my life, I went back to the dining room table, took the suicide note, and destroyed it.

That miracle kept me on my feet. I did not know what to do or say. After pacing the floor in unbelief, I decided to write to ORU. In the letter, I said I was excited and, by faith, I knew God would bring me there. I took the first step to enclose $100 for the room and board deposit. I continued to believe God was going to intervene again. *Even if I have no money, God will bring it just before I leave,* I reminded myself.

Somehow my faith was restored. I knew I would have the money to pay for my academic year. The devil's suggestions could no longer be accepted. He lost the war and all his tactics to destroy me failed. My spirit and faith in the God who never fails was alive once again.

The arrival of the letter at that particular time was perfect proof that God cared for me. He is always the same. He knows what is happening in our lives at all times.

"For the eyes of the Lord are on the righteous and his ears are attentive to their prayers, but the face of the Lord is against those who do evil." (1 Peter 3:12)

God is concerned about you. You are very special to Him. That is why He knows how many hairs are on your head, and He is the one who is saying to you, "Fear ye not; therefore, you are of more value than anything in the world," Matthew 10: 30-31. Who you are or what you can do for God is not what matters. Our focus must be on WHO HE IS because that is what really matters.

My weakness and my frustration did not alter God's plan for me. He had to accomplish His purpose for my life. Even when I was angry and bitter with Him, He still had the best plans for me. He knew my heart said, "Yes, Lord!" to His will. I had accepted Jesus as my Lord and Savior, and my life was consumed with living for Him and serving Him.

As a reader of this book, let me encourage you. In whatever situation you find yourself, look at the faithfulness of God rather than your problem or situation. But if you have somehow failed to trust Him, do not give up. Turn to Him. He is the only answer, and He will work things out for you.

> *"Trust in the Lord with all your heart and lean*
> *not on your own understanding; in all your*
> *ways acknowledge Him, and He will make*
> *your paths straight."* (Proverbs 3:5-6)

As soon as I mailed the response to the university, miracles started pouring in. Friends started praying for me and my faith continued to be renewed. I started planning to raise money for school. I told Pastor Stanley to announce in the church that I had some African crafts for sale. The money I raised would be used for the trip and for tuition. Although I knew what I had was not enough even to pay for a ticket, I had to take a step of faith and give all I had and believe God to do the rest.

I saw God's hand at work on my behalf. In one week, I managed to send over $2,000 for tuition. People started sending money from everywhere. I wondered how some of them heard about the trip. From different directions, cards came with money as condolences for the death of my mother. *Where have they been? My mother died in May,* I thought. I was back in Sweden in June and now it was almost the end of July and people were sending cards and money!

It did not make sense, but I knew God was at work on my behalf. I felt Him saying, "Do not worry about tomorrow, for tomorrow will worry about itself. Each day has enough trouble of its own," (Matthew 6:34).

The whole situation reminded me of the story in Luke 5:1-11, when Peter and the other fishermen toiled the whole night without catching any fish. When they had given up, ready to leave after cleaning their nets, Jesus stepped in and said, "Put out into deep water, and let down the nets for a catch." It was the same lake that they had toiled in all night. The only difference was now the Creator of the sea and all that dwells therein had spoken: "Let down the nets for a catch." The fish had been hiding from Peter, but now they had to rush into his net. The lake had to produce what was in it for Peter's benefit.

This story has a very important lesson for us to learn. The miracle of the fish happened after Peter gave an empty boat to be used by Jesus. Is your life empty? Turn it over to Jesus. He will fill your life with His miracles like he filled the empty boat. The disciples did not know what He was going to do with Peter's boat. They just gave it to Him. Jesus turned their sorrow into joy. He filled my empty life, even my pocketbook, and He can do the same for you. We serve a Living God who has never failed.

The miracles did not stop there. God intervened even with the post office. In Sweden, normally the mail was slow in the summer, but mail traveled quickly between Stockholm and Tulsa. In less than three weeks, I got the money, received the necessary papers from school, and obtained the visa from the American Embassy in Stockholm. My friends could not believe it, except to see God in every step. I left Sweden August 10, 1980, for the United States of America. God's supernatural intervention is beyond the understanding of my human mind. I just praise Him for who He is.

All the way on that trip, I felt I was heading to a divine appointment with God. My people in Tanzania did not know I left Sweden. Everything was done in a rush, and I had no motivation to write to them at that time. They were still in mourning. However, I was glad they would not be hearing that I was dead but rather I moved and changed continents. Indeed, God's ways are not our ways. We need to trust Him even if we do not understand. He is more concerned with our well being than we are.

After arriving in Tulsa, I tried to write my family several times; however, each time I tried, I would break down in tears and could not write. One day, I asked my roommate, who was from New York, to help me make an overseas call. She got the international operator, and I placed my call.

In a minute, I was connected with my family. "This is Nicku," I said and then kept silent. I was overcome by emotions. "I am in America," I said after awhile when I worked up the courage to speak again.

"Where?" My sister asked. "What are you doing in America?" For a long time, I could not say anything except to cry. Several of my family members came on the phone and asked the same thing. "God has brought me here to go to school, and I cannot understand anything," I replied. Tears filled my eyes, and I could not talk anymore. I put the phone down.

My roommate looked at me and said, "Nicku, that telephone call will cost you a fortune. You have been crying and wasting the time for over an hour. It will cost too much." At that time, I was not concerned with money. My thoughts and emotions were at home. I was visualizing my family being together without mother. It was very painful. However, I had hope that God was going to carry me through because I knew how He brought me there.

Academically, it was hard to understand American English. The devil tried to laugh at me, but I did not give him a chance. When I did not understand the lectures, I went into my closet to talk to Him, who had brought me to the university. God was all in all for me.

Surely enough, God was concerned with my every move at school. When the telephone bill arrived, there was no charge for the call I made to Tanzania. My roommate thought perhaps the telephone company would include it with our next bill. We waited; the second bill came, and there was no charge. We decided to call and ask the telephone company. I had the date and time of the call logged in my dairy, so it was easy to give them all the particulars. However, when they checked, the telephone company said it had no record of such a call made from our number.

My roommate was astonished. I was not amazed. I knew God performed another miracle on my behalf.

"... God is able to do immeasurably more than all we ask or imagine, according to his power that is at work within us. To Him be the glory...." (Ephesians 3:20-21)

"Nicku, this is America," my roommate said. "The computer never makes a mistake, especially when it concerns money. How did it happen?" She looked at me and continued, "I am sure they are just fooling you. They will send it when it has accumulated with the other overseas bills. Since you are from Africa, you do not understand our system."

"My God is above all technology," I said. "He performs miracles in the villages at home, and He is the one who performed miracles in Sweden. He can perform miracles even in the sophisticated American society as long as I continue to trust Him." She did not argue anymore.

Indeed, from 1980 until I finished school with a Doctor of Ministry degree in 1991, I can only say that I have seen the miracles of God throughout. I never took a job, nor did I receive a salary from anywhere. I was always busy witnessing or helping others and travelling to spread His love. My life is dedicated to God and helping others come to know Him.

Miraculously, God saw to it that every bill at school was paid through scholarships, gifts from people I never knew, and my church in Stockholm, who helped during my first degree. What the Scripture says in Matthew 6:33 is true—"Seek first his kingdom and his righteousness and all these things will be given to you as well." Just try and you will see the manifestation. I attended a private university and received three degrees without a loan or a job—that is God! He has given me more than I ever imagined.

Is there anything you desperately need? Trust God and follow His principles. You will be amazed at what God can do with you and through you. He is a good God!

I thank God for every miracle and every trial He brought me through. Above all, I thank Him for giving His all for me, for trusting me, and calling me to be His witness "in Jerusalem, in all Judea and Samaria and to the ends of the earth," as it says in Acts 1:8.

The way God took me away from home and sent me to Sweden was the same way He took me out of Sweden and brought me to the United States. Although I knew He wanted me to study, I never thought I could achieve a doctoral degree.

My intention was to finish a Bachelor of Arts degree and then return to my people. God had to prove over and over to me that He was not through with me in Oklahoma.

Year by year, God had to convince me to go on with school, and I did so out of obedience to Him.

Even my marriage was a surprise. I was not eager nor had any thought of marriage. I never spent time praying for a husband, but God knew what was best for me. Nevertheless, He had to prove to me that it was He who wanted me to be married. He provided a life partner for me, and I thank Him.

I have experienced God's love in more ways than I have written in this book. The more I fix my eyes on God's business, the more He cares and provides for me. There are many people who have been saved and touched through my life, and I give God the glory. Also, more things have been added to my life than I had ever thought or prayed for. Now I have a wonderful husband with two lovely children. Some friends have become like family to us. All glory and honor belong to God.

My life is sold out to God Almighty and to His mission. He knows where we will be tomorrow. Now I have stopped dictating to Him because I always lose. I have learned to trust and follow in His footsteps. Please pray for me, my family, and the ministry He has given me to enhance the Church. My desire is to live worthy of His calling and to "know Christ and the power of His resurrection, and the fellowship of sharing in His suffering, becoming like Him in His death…" (Philippians 3:10-11).

Thank you for reading this book. It is my prayer that you have been encouraged, and you will start having a blind faith to release your God-given potential. Above all, let me hear from you if this book has been a blessing. Indeed, it is a great thing to serve God and live for Him.

The Miracles Continue

Many years have passed since these miracles. There are also many more significant miraculous events that I have not included in this book. I continue to experience God's amazing miracles in my life and ministry. The latter has expanded considerably since those early years. I go on mission trips to Africa several times a year. Sometimes this even includes taking a team with me on medical missions to some of the most remote places in Africa. Each time I go, I see the miraculous hand of God provide for these trips. With each passing year, I discover more and more of His great love for the world and for mankind and become more aware of His personal love and care for me.

I was reminded of that on a particular trip that included Liberia, Ivory Coast, Chad, and Niger. I remember thinking before I left about how much I was looking forward to enjoying some of the delicious mangoes of Africa. So, naturally, every country I went I requested some mangoes. But due to our busy schedule, it did not look like I was going to have that pleasure.

En route to return to the USA, we had a long layover in Abijan. Once again, I began lamenting that I did not get any mangoes. Two pastors who knew how much I was longing to enjoy mangoes from home went into town to see what they could find. I stayed at the airport with the luggage, waiting to get some mangoes before I left West Africa. After an hour or so, one team member returned and gave me a bag of fruits. I was so happy. I positioned myself to open the bag and start eating them. I even had my wet paper towels ready to wash the fruits so I could eat them right there. But as I opened the bag, I found papayas, not mangoes.

"These are not mangoes. How could you do that to me?" I said, quite frustrated.

"This is what Pastor Moussa bought for you," the young man said politely. Although I appreciated the effort and did not want to appear ungracious or unthankful, I simply could not eat those papayas. I wanted my African mangoes!

When we arrived at Dulles airport in Virginia, I was still disappointed about not getting those mangoes. When my husband and daughter came to pick me up, I did not talk about the miracles God performed on the trip. I did not talk about the many people who received Jesus as their Savior. The only thing I talked about was how sad I was that I did not get to eat mangoes from home. I even told them of my further disappointment when the young man at Abijan airport brought me papayas instead of mangoes.

As we arrived home and pulled in the driveway, my daughter noticed a box by our door.

"It was not there before we left to pick up Mommy," my husband told Edith, who was inquiring about the box. "Go see what is in it!"

I did not pay much attention to the box. I was too tired to be curious, but my daughter ran to open it nonetheless.

"Mommy! MANGOES!" she yelled as soon as she had it open.

All the tiredness instantly disappeared. We all rushed to the box to see. There were twelve mangoes! Twelve beautiful, African mangoes, nothing like the ones we could buy at the international stores here. These mangoes looked like they had been freshly picked from the mango trees in Africa! In that moment, I felt God's love wash all over me.

At the same time, my heart felt conviction over my earlier complaints and attitude. Yet, it was as if God was saying, "My daughter, you are not just My servant; you are My child! I care for your personal needs and desires as much as I care for the world to which I send you! You are Mine!"

God feels the same way about everyone reading this book. He is near to all who call upon Him.

CPSIA information can be obtained at www.ICGtesting.com
Printed in the USA
BVOW04s1855271013

334722BV00008B/19/P